felt

New Directions for an Ancient Craft

Gunilla Paetau Sjöberg

Translated by Patricia Spark

INTERWEAVE PRESS

Ingram 24.95

FELT
New Directions for an Ancient Craft
by Gunilla Paetau Sjöberg

Translation, Patricia Spark

Photography, Gunilla Paetau Sjöberg 14, 15, 16 left and upper right, 18, 23, 24, 25, 26, 27, 28, 29, 30, 31, 33, 35 bottom, 36, 39 right, 40, 41, 46 right, 48, 49, 50, 51, 56, 57, 60, 64, 65, 66, 67 top, 68, 69, 70, 71, 72, 73, 75, 76, 78, 80, 84, 86, 87, 88 lower left, 89, 94, 95, 97, 98, 101, 102, 103, 104 left column, 107 upper right, 109, 110, 111, 112, 113, 114, 117, 118, 119, 122, 123, 124, 125, 127 top, 129, 130, 131 left column, 133, 134, 135, 136, 137, 138, 139, 140, 146, 147; Bo Gyllander 81, 83, 85 top; Birjer Johnsson 104 top and middle: Yoichi Nishimura 105 middle and right, 106, 107 left and middle; Hermitage, St. Petersburg 6, 7, 8; T Shugiyama/D Chulunbator 9; Benrido, Kyoto 10, 11; Gösta Montell 28 upper right; The National Archeological Museum of Christian-Albrechts University, Schloß Gottorf Sleswick 17; Nordiska Museum's Picture Archives 19; Katarina Ågren 20; Meyer/Weum AS 21 left; Samuli Paulaharju, Museum of Industry, Helsinki 22 right; Mari Nagy 34, 35 top, 91 bottom; Inger Monson 39 lower left; Patricia Spark 46 left; Andreas Davidsson 45, 85 left, 132, 142, 143; Inge Evers 46 right; Lennart Falk 52; Martin Hallén 67 left; Doug Kyle 77; Maj-Britt Lundaahl 82 bottom right; Marianne Davidson Ekert 88 right; Lars Elenius 91 upper right; Gerald Sedgewick 91 upper left; Veli Vanhanen 93 left; Per Nybø 92 left; Pekka Turtiainen 92 right; Silja Puranen 93 right; Jorie Johnson 150 upper left; The Class Studio in Ed 107 lower right; Torolf Engen 108; Lópata 116; Lars Ödmark 127 left; Mika Mäntyniemi 131 lower right; Stephanie Bunn 144, 145.

Illustration, Mona Rönningen
Production, Marc McCoy Owens
Cover design, Elizabeth R. Mrofka
Cover art, Anne Sneary

Interweave Press, Inc.
201 East Fourth Street
Loveland, Colorado 80537
USA

printed in Hong Kong by Sing Cheong

Library of Congress Cataloging-in-Publication Data
    Sjöberg, Gunilla Paetau.
        [Tova. English]
        Felt : new directions for an ancient craft / by Gunilla Paetau
    Sjöberg.
            p.   cm.
        Translation of: Tova.
        Includes index.
        ISBN 1-883010-17-9
        1. Felting.   2. Felt work.   I. Title
    TT849.5.S5613   1996
    746'.0463—dc20   96-10562
                                                        CIP

First printing:IWP—7.5M:496:CC

Contents

Foreword

This book was inspired by the creative work in an uncommonly useful technique, felting. During the past fifteen years, the knowledge, method, design, and functional possibilities have grown in a thrilling way. Anything can be shaped from wool—clothing, functional textiles, toys, jewelry, and art. Wool is a common, abundant natural resource, which in an important consideration in this age of ecological sensitivity.

In the past, handmade felt has played an important role in human survival and it is still used for tents, carpets, and clothing by the Central Asiatic nomads. According to archeological discoveries from this area, the tradition is derived from an archaic, artistically advanced felt culture. In addition to the Central Asiatic technique, this book also explores felting in the Nordic countries and Europe, and the techniques and designs of Kashmir, Turkmenistan, and Turkey.

Although the felting process has its roots way back in time, the technique was almost unknown in Sweden when Katarina Ågren's book, *Tovning,* (Felting) was published in 1976. When I first read the book, I was reminded of the Finnish boots of my youth which, though factory made, were made of felted wool, and were similar to the felt socks made by hand in Västerbotten.

What a technique! A wet, shapeless pile of wool could be felted into a well-fitting sock in half an hour! And without any special equipment! As I learned that the wool was simply massaged gently and then brutally rubbed on what looked to be an antique wash board, my curiosity grew. And I was excited by the potential of the technique as an artistic medium—a felted sculpture could embrace the character of the natural material.

During the past few years, the felting process has become widespread. In Sweden as well as other countries, courses in felting have been added to the curriculum in textile departments, and the technique is now used by many artists and craftspeople. Swedish felting techniques have spread to Hungary, North America, and other countries both east and west. At the same time, felting methods were taken up in Europe and the United States. Mary E. Burkett arranged the first large felt exhibition in England in 1979. The well-documented catalog from this exhibit showed how felt was used in different parts of the world where it was still considered a handcraft.

Contact has also been made between feltmakers in different countries. For this, special thanks go to Mari Nagy and István Vidák. For several years, they organized international workshops on the Hungarian Pusta (Hungarian Prairie), and inspired many young Hungarian students to study the true feltmaking countries in Central Asia. Ottó Farkas listened to them, and I am indebted to him for making it possible for me to meet the true felt artists—the Mongolian nomads.

In Småland in 1991, ABF (The Education Organization) and Marianne Ekert organized an international felt festival. In the same summer, a large symposium was organized in Denmark by Annette Damgaard and Lene Nielsen. Both events were forums for the exchange of knowledge and ideas between felt enthusiasts from different countries. Felt Associations have been started in England, Denmark, Norway, the United States, Australia, and New Zealand. These groups publish newsletters, and arrange courses and exhibits.

The technique has found its rightful place on the artistic plane. In the Nordic Textile Triennial 1992–1993, there were five felted works from three Nordic countries.

On the technical plane, the process has grown considerably. It has evolved, been refined, and broadened. Knowledge of the Central Asiatic rolling methods has made it possible for large pieces of felt cloth to be made for clothing, upholstery fabric, and large carpets without incurring broken backs and aching wrists.

Space limitations have necessitated that this book focus on the different felting techniques and uses, although there is much more to be said about the history of felt and the felting process in different countries.

The humble felt sock and its use over the years in many cultures is also discussed—the sock has been seen on horse back, in lumber work, and even on our feet as we watch television. Perhaps this symbolizes all feltmakers who lived before us, who helped their people to survive a cold climate, and who now give us the foundation to appreciate well-felted everyday items and personal expression.

I am proud to present many of my felting friends, course participants, and students through pictures of their work—thanks to you all for the generous contributions. I would also like to thank Katarina Ågren, Alan Waller, Ingvar Svanberg, to name just a few, for reviewing parts of the text, and Mia Fallman, my apprentice, who patiently modeled garments. Lastly, I would like to thank my family, who have had to put up with a lot of wool over the course of the years!

—*Gunilla Paetau Sjöberg*

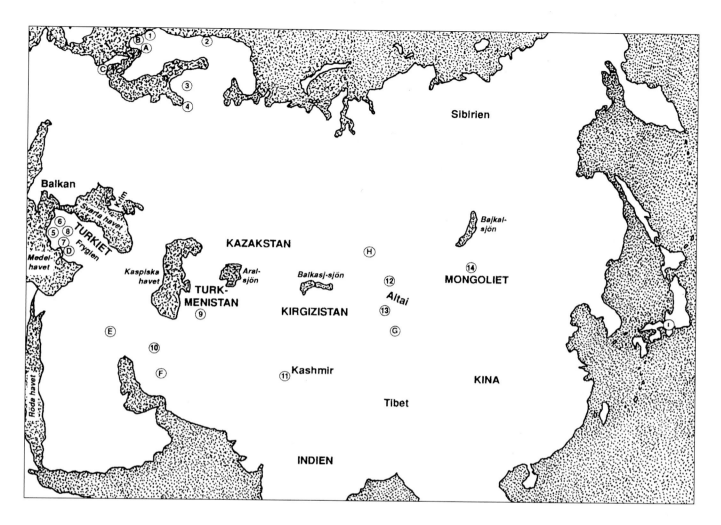

Map of felt discoveries showing both the modern and the ancient places named in this book.

Felt has its origins in Asia and Europe and came to North America by way of European millinery. Many natives of South American countries still wear felt hats, a custom they adopted from Spanish conquerors. Felt most likely came to the Muslim countries of North Africa from the East during the eighth century. In Ethiopia, saddle felts and woven, fulled mantles are still produced.

Sites of the oldest finds and their ancient names:

A. Oseberg
B. Hordaland
C. Hedeby
D. Çatal Hüyük
E. Babylon
F. Persepolis
G. Noin Ula
H. Pazyryk
I. Nara

Contemporary Names:

1. Haus
2. Nesna
3. Jämsä
4. St. Petersburg
5. Tire
6. Kula
7. Konya
8. Afyon
9. Ashabad
10. Isfahan
11. Srinagar
12. Manhan
13. Bulgan
14. Ulan Bator

Felt Discoveries in Asia

Many stories have been told about how feltmaking was discovered. One of these dates back to the story of Noah's Ark. The sheep in the ark were underfed and placed in cramped, warm quarters. They shed their wool onto the floor beneath them, urinated on the fallen fiber, and trampled on it with their hooves. When the sheep left the ark, they left behind a felted rug! This simple story describes how wool becomes felt—wool, alkaline moisture (i.e., urine), and agitation (from the sheep's trampling) are all that are needed.

Researchers believe that felt is one of the earliest textile forms, but because it is a material that decomposes easily, artifacts are scarce.

Feltmaking likely began in Asia, where it is an important part of folk tradition that has developed into an art form. Contemporary feltmakers will find a wealth of inspiration from both the new and the old Asian felt techniques. Information about the ancient techniques comes from the Pazyryk discoveries in Siberia.

The Pazyryk Discoveries

In 1929, two scientists from Russia found felt objects in the Altai highlands of Siberia, Asia. Their excavations yielded objects dated to 600–200 B.C. from a grave in a Pazyryk burial site situated more than 1,600 meters (5,250 feet) above sea level. Four other grave excavations in the same region were made between 1947 and 1949 under the direction of Russian archaeologist Sergei I. Rudenko and are recounted in his book, *The Frozen Tombs of Siberia*.

Felt mosaic from 400 B.C. This is a detail from a large wall covering or carpet. 4.5 × 6.5 m (15 × 21 ft). The textile was found in Pazyryk kurgan 5 in the Altai mountains. The same motif, a goddess who is waited upon by a horseman, repeats across the entire surface in double rows and abuts the border. Hermitage, St. Petersburg, Russia.

The grave chambers of Pazyryk, called *kurgan*, were located in an area of permafrost (frozen ground), which protected objects that otherwise would not have survived. Centuries ago, water seeped into the chamber and froze, preserving the grave's contents in ice. When the ice was melted, the ancient nomadic lifestyle was revealed.

The Altai people's magnificent burials were similar to those of the nearby Scythians. The grave chamber was constructed from timber in the bottom of a large, deep hole. The chamber had double walls adorned with felt hangings. A coffin with an embalmed body was placed on the floor, and the chamber was filled with utilitarian objects and the possessions of the deceased. A line of fully outfitted horses, a two-wheeled wagon, and other equipment were placed outside the chamber. The grave was carefully covered with layers of leaves and bark, followed by a timber roof, dirt, and finally a large stone cairn.

Among the burial artifacts were livestock and small adult horses from Altai herds, pelts, gold, and silver. Although the Altai tribes lived in isolated areas, the finds indicate connections with other groups: thoroughbred saddle horses from Central Asia, embroidered silk from China, wool clothing of typical Iranian style, and beautiful woven carpets. The graves also reveal that mixed marriages existed between peoples of the Altai region—the Pazyryk had a European type of body structure, but the graves also held bodies with Mongolian and Indo-European characteristics.

Material resources

The Altai people's own creative handwork is remarkable in its richness and multiplicity of techniques and materials. All of the finds give evidence of a highly developed culture with exceptional technical and design skills. These nomadic people surrounded themselves with beautiful forms and decorated functional items. Natural resources must have been rich. Domesticated and wild animals provided materials for felt, leather, and furs of the highest quality. Larch and cedar trees were used for woodcarving. Dyes from henna, indigo, and madder came from the plant world, while mineral colors such as ochre and cinnabar were derived from the earth. Precious metals were plentiful, as evidenced by the generous use of gold and silver decorations on utilitarian goods.

Felt objects

Among the objects of ceramic, wood, leather, gold, furs, and textiles were many felt pieces. Rudenko's findings included wall hangings, shrouds, coffin linings, boots for men and women, stockings, pillows stuffed with deer hair, small felt-covered rings used to hold round-bottomed vessels upright, outdoor garments for men, and hair rats (felt lumps over which hair is rolled) for women. Felt decorations were found on blankets, saddles, bows, bridles, saddle blankets, masks and bits for horses, and the interiors and exteriors of tents.

The Altai men were dressed in shirts of hemp fiber, caftans of skin or felt, and pants of soft leather. They wore felt stockings and high leather boots with soft soles. On their heads were tall caps with earflaps. The women wore cloaks of squirrel skin lined with fur and short, fur-edged boots, also with soft soles. Their clothing was decorated with appliqué and mosaics of dyed felt, skin, and leather. Some were embroidered with wool and sinew thread wrapped with metal foil. The felt was in a variety of thicknesses, depending on its use. Many of the felt techniques used by the Altai people are still used today, 2,500 years later, by the feltmakers of Central Asia.

Design and technique

The Altai felting style resembles the Scythian animal style (also called the Scythian-Siberian animal style). The motifs were predominantly animals and birds, both wild and tame, which were stylized and shaped to fit the objects being decorated. The designers excelled at elegant compositions. To fit their needs, they gracefully lengthened or shortened animals' bodies, bent the heads and backs into curves, and strengthened the expressive qualities of the animals they reproduced. The

Saddle blanket, 400 B.C., from Pazyryk kurgan 1, Altai mountains. 119 × 60 cm (46 × 23 in). This saddle blanket is typical in terms of style, technique, and material combinations. The bodies of the stylized fighting animals are appliquéd with a couched edge. Some of the leather details have gold foil decorations. Blue fur and a fringe of red horsehair embellish the flaps. Iron Age horsemen had wonderful trappings for their horses: a felt blanket was laid under the saddle, and a magnificent cover such as this was placed on top of the saddle.

Detail of a felt shabrack with cut edge. 400 B.C., Pazyryk kurgan 5, Altai.

Stuffed swan, sewn from pieces, 400–300 B.C., Pazyryk kurgan 5 in the Altai mountains. Length 35 cm (14 in). Four swans, all slightly different, were perched on the corners of a canopy-covered wooden wagon. The swans' legs were stiffened with wooden ribs.

Felt shabrack (cavalry saddle cloth), 400 B.C., Pazyryk kurgan 5, Altai mountains. Hanging from the bottom of the cloth are braided woolen cords with wooden dangles representing flower buds.

Felt appliqué on a covering, Pazyryk kurgan 1, Altai. The lion's head is repeated with red and blue alternating in the middle of a border formed from red, blue, yellow, and white triangles.

designs were dynamic and displayed power and energy.

Researchers disagree on whether the Altai style was influenced by the Scythians or the two experienced parallel development. For us, newcomers to feltwork, the Altai felt art is a source of endless inspiration for design and sewing techniques, and offers a free approach to blending materials. The Altai adorned felt with cloth, fur, leather, horsehair, pelts, sinew, and metals. They laid leather next to felt in mosaic work, used fine sinew thread wrapped with metal foil to couch seams between textile surfaces, and placed horsehair tufts between layers of felt to make fringes. Women's felt boots were edged with fur and extensively adorned with lines of embroidery and beads. Wood, birch bark, bone, horn, feathers, and shells were combined with felt, which in some cases also contained human hair. Sculptures, plates, and ornaments in silver and gold were appliquéd to felt. Holes were sometimes cut out of felt to reveal layers of different colors or a leather backing.

Rudenko's book includes many illustrations, and I recommend it for more information and inspiration. Pieces from his unique felt discovery can be viewed at the Hermitage Museum in St. Petersburg, Russia. The felt objects are located in the Pazyryk room. The Museum of Ethnography in St. Petersburg has an interesting collection of felt objects as well, which date from the past two centuries.

Noin-Ula Finds

Another grave chamber found in the Noin Ula mountains of Mongolia was 1,500 meters (4,920 feet) above sea level. Located in a shaft 10 meters (33 feet) deep, it contained felt objects that date to the first century, including two carpets decorated with appliqué in felt. The larg-er carpet measures 2.60 by 1.96 meters (8½ by 6½ feet) and has a monochromatic center field decorated with twenty-four spiral shapes. The area between the spirals is filled with tonguelike swirls. All of these patterns were made by quilting. (It is interesting to note that the majority of felt carpets made in Mongolia today are decorated with the same technique and pattern forms.) A simple border runs around the carpet's center field, which is in turn bordered with a frieze of alternating tree symbols and animals attacking one another. Rudenko noted that some of the artifacts found in this grave chamber—a pointed cap and a pair of women's shoes—are similar to those found at Pazyryk.

Rug with felt appliqué and quilting, first century, Noin Ula, Mongolia. 2.60 × 1.96 m (8½ × 6½ ft). National museum, Ulan Bator, Mongolia.

Shōsō-In Treasures

Along with many other precious items, some felt rugs are deposited in an emperor's treasure chamber in Nara, Japan. One rug is thought to have come from China or Korea; another is believed to have come from Korea sometime between A.D. 668 and 918. These rugs are remarkable not because they are artifacts discovered in an archaeological dig, but because they have been stored for more than 1,200 years! In ancient Japan, all of the emperor's palaces included separate buildings for the treasure chambers. The Shōsō-in is one of the last of these to be built, and it is dated to A.D. 756. It includes a large variety of more than 9,000 objects, the majority being from the Tang period (A.D. 618–906). The objects are preserved in the favorable conditions of the dark chamber. Once each year, the treasure chamber is opened so that the objects can be aired and placed in an exhibit arranged by the national museum in Nara.

The treasure chamber houses thirty patterned rugs, called *kasen,* in various sizes. The rugs have a variety of inlaid patterns made with felt and dyed wool. One rug, decorated with a flower pattern in the shape of palmettos, is Western in style. Another is decorated with landscape elements and a motif of two parrots holding flowers in their beaks. According to the book *Mattor från Kina, Siankiang och Tibet,* by Lennart Larsson, Jr., one rug is ornamented in classic Tang style with flowers, graceful leaves, and clouds in various forms. The pattern is blue, green, yellow, and red on a natural white background.

Felt rug. Shōsō-in collection, Nara, Japan. 240 × 130 cm (94 × 51 in). The background color is pale yellow, and the pattern is blue gray.

Other sources of historical felt information

Information on felt can also be researched in historical texts and pictorial depictions that refer to its traditions, distribution, technical descriptions, and uses. For instance, the books by Katarina Ågren (*Tovning*) and Mary E. Burkett (*The Art of the Felt Maker*) offer many interesting facts and theories.

In historical references, there are many statements about the use of felt in the military. Presumably, early people discovered that thick felt offered protection against both weapons and weather.

By 2300 B.C., Chinese warriors were outfitted with felt shields, head coverings, clothing, and shoes. Felt is still used extensively in China, and felt rugs are common in the northern part of the country. The Chinese probably learned to felt from the nomadic people of Central Asia. Traders' caravans crossed Mongolia, the political boundaries changed, and Chinese noblewomen were married to Mongol nobles to strengthen the ties between the countries. There is considerable documentation of Chinese felt production from the time of Mongolian rule. For example, in A.D. 1299, 331 square meters (3,563 square feet) of felt carpet were made in Ninghsia for the harem in the emperor's palace.

Felt rug. Shōsō-in collection, Nara, Japan. 244 × 130 cm (95 × 51 in). The background is pale yellow, the pattern, blue gray with light green in the leaves.

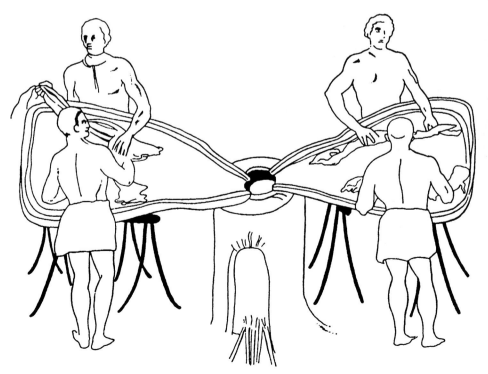

Feltmaking wall painting outside Verecundus's factory in Pompeii. The technique of slanting the worktable so that it drains down to a kettle over a wood fire is still in use in Hungary.

Felt Traditions in Europe and Southwest Asia

There is evidence that felt was used as early as 6000 B.C., even in the western world. In Çatal Hüyük, Turkey, researchers have found fragments of felt as well as evidence of spinning and weaving. Mary E. Burkett believes that the painting on the grave chamber wall is of images of felt wall hangings. The patterns in the painting are very similar to those traditionally found on felt, not woven, textiles. This theory is supported by the fact that felt artifacts were found at the site.

An understanding of early felt use can be gained through literary sources and pictorial representations. Many historians and authors have written about felt.

In A.D. 400, Herodotus wrote about the Scythians' felt-covered tents. About 100 years later, the geographer Strabo wrote about the Scythians' felt-covered wagons. According to Herodotus, one Scythian tribe also used thick white felt to shield fruit trees. Scythians are the first nomadic people known to have found their way north of the Black Sea on the Russian steppes. They inhabited the area about 700 B.C. and are legendary for their art of warfare. Over time, they became increasingly more settled but maintained a lively contact with other people.

Caps and Hats

Information on head coverings can be found in many written accounts. Throughout the ages and in all cultures that utilize textiles, head coverings have been made of felt. No other material offers felt's malleability, density, and ability to hold its shape. Even the ancient Babylonians wore felt caps. Strabo tells of high caps that looked like towers. There are also cap images on the reliefs found at Persepolis (see map on page 5).

In the *Iliad*, Homer mentions felt caps, and in the *Odyssey*, Odysseus's felt-lined helmet. The Greeks learned the technique from the Asiatic people with whom they traded. They manufactured coats for soldiers, rain capes, and, especially, head coverings. A dense cap became the fashion among fishermen and artisans. The Greek word for felt is *pilos*.

The Romans learned feltmaking from the Greeks. Roman soldiers wore tight felt caps, even when going to the theater and dining! Felt armor manufactured in Rome was dipped in vinegar to make it resistant to both fire and iron weapons. In addition to felt head coverings and armor, Roman soldiers wore felt boots and stockings.

The felt cap came to be seen as a symbol of freedom in ancient Rome. It was the custom for freed slaves to shave their heads and wear a felt cap, called a *pileus*, as a sign of their freedom. The phrase *ad pileum vocare* (to be called to the felt cap), referred to the slaves' agitation for freedom. In those times, all fishermen, workers, and artisans wore felt caps. The caps came to be associated with the masses or the "felt mob", as the historian Suetonius called the large crowd of joyous people who fled out of the Roman gates after Nero died.

During the French Revolution in 1792, caps were again used as symbols of freedom. At the time, the Jacobins (the radical political club that played a controlling part in the revolution) wore Phrygian-style caps with peaks that bent forward. These caps are represented in Delacroix's painting *Freedom Leading the People* as well as on seals and stamps.

The professional manufacture of hats has long been a tradition in many countries. The first hatmaking guild statutes in Germany were written in the town of Lübeck in 1321. Nordic journeymen traveled to Germany to learn hatmaking. The German hatmakers also manufactured felt socks.

In many Balkans countries, Asia Minor, and Southwest Asia, felt caps are still in use. They are both machine made and handmade at small felt factories.

The Phrygian cap, after a sculpture in the museum in Selçuk, Turkey. In different times and lands, the Phrygian-style cap has been worn in different ways.

A Jacobin at a barricade during the French Revolution wears a freedom symbol, the Phrygian cap. This version is red and somewhat fuller and freely crushed, judging by the paintings of Fragonard and Delacroix. The works of these artists give a suggestion of the republican dress adopted by extreme Jacobins.

Parade of historical hats. From left to right: Median courtier, Babylonian, Scythian from 500 B.C., two Phoenicians from A.D. 800.

Wide-brimmed and plumed felt hat, initially made popular during the Baroque period (1600–1750), later called a *Rubens* or *Rembrandt* hat.

Dancing dervish with a *sikke,* the ritual high felt hat. The dance and the hat's height help establish contact with a higher power. Dervish words have been found in Turkey since A.D. 1200. During prayer, the dervishes use a smaller felt cap called an *arakiye.*

The *tricorne,* with the brim formed into three corners was in fashion during the reign of Louis XIV. This style came into use as military attire during the seventeenth and eighteenth centuries. It was also worn by the Swedish militia during World War I.

Feltmaker, Mehmet Girgiç, in Konya. He still makes the dervish *sikke* out of soft mohair called *tiftik.* Previously, camel hair was used, but now it is difficult to obtain. The hat is felted like a closed bag that is folded in the middle, thus making it double. The tall sides are stiffened with a solution of sugar water.

The *fez* or *tarboosh* was commanded by the Ottoman empire to be worn by all nationalities in 1832. It was worn by Muslims of both genders. It was made of smooth wool felt and was usually dyed red, but could be black. The tassel on a man's fez could be black or blue silk. A woman's fez could have gold or bead embroidery, and was worn under a veil.

A Hungarian Hatmaker

The tradition of hand-felting hats has been lost in most of Europe. But in Hungary, Zoltán Mihalkó continues the craft he learned from his father. He is now taking his turn as a teacher so that the tradition will continue.

1. Zoltán Mihalkó makes six hats in two days. On the first day, he loosens the fleece with a carding bow suspended from the ceiling and lays the wool out into two bell-shaped piles (called hat blanks) for each hat. On the second day, he felts both hats.

Only the finest Merino lamb's fleece is used. The locks are 2 cm (3/4 in) long and are scoured. The gut string of the carding bow is plucked to make it vibrate over the pile of fleece. "The ewes cast off their lamb's wool," says Zoltán. For each hat blank, 200 g (7 oz) of fleece is bow-carded twice. A little extra wool is also used to strengthen the outer layers of the hat's crown.

2. After being loosened, each of the two portions of fleece are formed into a bell shape with a basketlike tool and then flattened with a hatter's sieve (pictured). The materials are then folded up and stored until the work resumes the next day.

3. On the second day, the materials for two hats and the fleece reserved for strengthening their crowns are unfolded and placed between layers of cotton cloth. The pocket is wrapped in burlap and pinned together with large nails.

4. The work begins outdoors at a wood stove equipped with a built-in kettle and hearthstone. The fleece/cotton cloth packet is laid on the warm hearthstone and is sprinkled with water and covered with a doubled burlap bag to protect Zoltán's hands from the steam. The resulting steam is pressed down into the wool until all the fleece is flattened.

5. Back inside the building, the packet is opened, and the outer layer of the fleece pile is pressed down with the hatter's sieve. Templates are cut out of newspaper. The first half of the flattened fleece for a hat is folded around a template. The template is turned over and the other half is folded in the same way. Small wrinkles are eased out and the joint is covered with a thin layer of wool. The hat is held against the light to check for evenness. A sheet of paper is placed inside the hat's opening. The same is done for the second hat. Then cloth and sacking are wrapped around them. Outside on the warm hearthstone, the packets are steamed, pressed down, and turned over.

6. After steaming, each hat is opened and rotated so that the folds from the first side come to the middle of the bell shape. The side flaps created by these folds are stretched out and the hat crown is folded down into the hat. It is all placed inside cloth and sacking and is once again taken out to the hearthstone to be steamed and pressed down.

7. Next comes fulling and shaping. The work is moved to the other side of the large hearth where a special felting table has been set up. Raised edges and a slope on the table lead the water from the fulling back down into the kettle. Sulfuric acid (H_2SO_4) is added to the water (about 30 ml (2 tblsp) to 50 to 70 l (13 to 18½ gal) of water).

8. The hat is rolled back and forth from different directions around a wooden rolling pin. It is then blocked on a wooden form and the crown is worked down. A cord is wrapped twice around the crown line and drawn in to crimp in the excess width and allow the brim to extend beyond the crown. Then the brim is stretched and fulled until it takes the right shape.

9. Zoltán Mihalkó in his fulled hat. The dyeing, stiffening, and finishing comes later—work that is his wife's responsibility.

Mantles—An Ancient Garment

Felt mantles are found in countries that enjoy more varied felt production than is typical of herding populations. These mantles are still used in many countries in Asia Minor and Southwest Asia. They are often made in one piece without seams and may have felted-on hoods such as the Anatolian mantles, called *kepeneks,* do. Herders use their mantles both as one-person tents and as sleeping bags while they are in the fields tending to their animals. Sometimes, small lambs are given shelter in a mantle. Mantles have also been common in military attire.

Throughout time, mantles have been used by the highest social classes as ritual garments and as signs of special status. Mantles were given to important officials during state visits. For example, during the Middle Ages, herdsmen's mantles were given by the Arabian court to important visitors.

The richly embroidered mantles of Afghanistan have more of a social function than a practical one. The handsome Hungarian mantle, the *szür,* is made of heavily fulled woven wool fabric. It is generally accepted that such fulled fabrics are but a variation of felt. These mantles are richly decorated with embroidery and appliqué and were often used in courtship. After a girl's hand was requested, the boy's courtship mantle was left in her home overnight. If the mantle was hanging outside the next day on the house wall for the whole village to see, the young man would know that the answer was "no"!

Felt mantles are often heavily fulled, a technique we can apply when making similar garments. For example, stable and durable edges are produced by either cutting the opening after fulling or by sewing the cut opening with strong string before fulling. (The stitches are ripped out when the fulling is finished.) Mantles are made both with and without sleeves. If the felt is very thick and heavily fulled, the sleeves do not bend easily and are used for only decorative purposes. Consequently, some sleeves are only rudimentary. They are very small and difficult to impossible to put arms through. Some are so long that they can be tied behind the back. In villages near Isfahan in Iran, the sleeves are felted together along the bottom edge—clearly these sleeves were never intended to be used. In other villages in Iran, the sleeves are used only after the felt has had time to soften.

This mantle has the owner's initials and mantle size. Approximately 5.5 kg (12 lb) of wool, in alternating layers of lamb and adult fleece, are used for one mantle.

Felt Discoveries in the Nordic Countries

The majority of the ancient Nordic felt discoveries are fragments. However, from writings and pictures, we can draw conclusions about how felt was used. The oldest Nordic discovery comes from Hordaland, Norway, and dates to nomadic times, A.D. 400–500. The discovery includes two felt pieces that were wrapped around a dead man's leg and put into a bronze urn in a funeral pyre. The felt pieces are porous, 0.5 to 1 centimeter (1/5 to 2/5 inch) thick and 35 to 40 centimeters (14 to 15³/₄ inches) in diameter. It is believed that they were made in Norway and that the metal urn conserved the felt pieces.

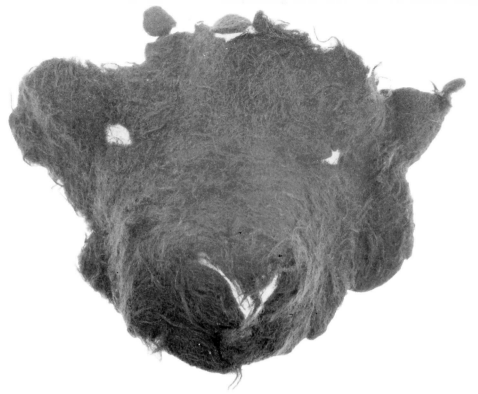

The Hedeby mask. The felt mask is 19 × 14 cm (7¹/₂ × 5¹/₂ in). The felt is 0.4 cm (1/6 in) thick and is dyed a reddish brown with walnut hulls. The mouth opening was cut in a point so that the nostrils would rise when the mask was sewn together farther down. The felt is tattered and shaggy on the surface. National Archaeological Museum, Schloß Gottorf, Schleswig, Germany.

Hedeby Mask from Viking Times

As recently as 1979, felt objects from Viking times were discovered in the northernmost region of Germany. One such item is a small felt face mask from a shipwreck in the harbor of the ancient town of Hedeby (also called Haithabu), which borders Denmark. Hedeby, which in Viking times belonged to Denmark, was an important trade center that had contact with all of the Scandinavian centers of the period.

The felt mask was totally saturated with tar and, along with other textile materials, was used to caulk the Viking boat. The tar protected the wool. The mask was not made to actually fit the head; it is merely in the form of a face mask or half mask. It resembles an animal, perhaps a sheep or bear. Among the outer layer of the caulking material was another mask that resembled a calf. This mask was woven and fulled, and sized to fit an adult.

Along with the masks, several small felt fragments were discovered. They appear to be scraps from pieces cut out of larger articles. The fragments are of different qualities; soft and hard, thin and thick, and some are two-colored. These variations indicate a mastery of felting techniques.

Inga Hägg, Ph.D., who is responsible for scientific research of the discovery, used linguistic and iconographic data to conclude that the masks were used along with other clothing disguises during ceremonies such as tournament play, in which the animal shapes would have great magical and symbolic meaning. She mentions that an example of this phenomenon is pictured on a Viking wall hanging discovered in Oseberg, Norway. The figure is wearing a pig mask.

In microscopic examination of the wool fibers in the small mask, the Danish feltmaker Annette Damgaard discovered that the inner fibers have a large range of thickness, which suggests an archaic sheep type. She points out that the fleece in the felt fragments is oriented in tufts, which may mean that the wool was beaten with sticks in the same manner that wool is currently prepared in Mongolia. The theories about the use of beating to process the wool are supported by Gertrud Grenander Nyberg, Ph.D., who has linked the masks to the discovery in Elisenhof, near Hedeby, of a flexible stick of hazel, which could be a beating stick for wool and which is about 200 years older than the Hedeby finds.

Another discovery from these times was made in the town of Mölnar, Väte parish, on Gotland. The felt scraps from this site, which are brown and measure 10 by 3 centimeters (4 by 1¹/₄ inches), were attached to the back side of a belt that has an Asian-style heart-shaped metal mount. The materials have not been tested in detail, and therefore the origin cannot be ascertained.

Felt from Later Times

In her book *Tovning*, Katarina Ågren mapped Nordic felt traditions in Norway, Sweden, and Finland from about 300 years ago to the present. In Denmark and on the Faeroe Islands, there is no known felt craft tradition. Felt was made earlier on Iceland, though no Icelandic felting tradition has survived. In the Icelandic sagas, there are references to felt, and some later writings tell of how felt saddles were made. Strong felt saddles have been preserved, and it appears that they were used alone, without other saddles over them.

The felting tradition in Nordic countries evolved through the need for simple utilitarian objects for life in a cold climate and an often stringent economy. It is also in the northern parts of the Nordic countries that felting developed as a home craft. However, by the 1960s, the craft of felting risked being forgotten in Finland, Norway, and Sweden.

Katarina Ågren's book contributed to the revival of felting instruction in Sweden, and today the technique is being taught and used over the entire country. Interest quickly spread to other countries, and *Tovning* was translated into Finnish and Dutch, and even awakened an interest in feltmaking in Hungary. In a short time, the Scandinavian felting methods had spread to North America as well as other countries.

Sweden

Traditionally, felting did not exist as a home craft south of Hälsingland. Most felting was done in Västerbotten, Jämtland, and Ångermanland.

In the early 1960s, Katarina Ågren, then an antiquarian with the Västerbotten museum, and the home-craft consultant Karin Lundholm began to study archaic felting techniques. By this time,

indoor heating and the availability of commercially made warm footwear had put feltmaking on the road to extinction. These studies revitalized felting, not just in northern Sweden but throughout the country. Artists, artisans, craftspeople, and hobbyists began to use the technique in many different ways. Teachers began to teach feltmaking and expose modern children to ancient techniques.

Socks

Historically, socks have been the most common felt product. Cozy to wear in a cold and drafty house, they could also be worn for short trips outdoors. Felt socks were worn as liners in low work boots, and in ski boots and high walking boots during the winter. In extreme cold, children have been known to wear felted socks over their boots.

Felt socks are still used today. I recently met a forty-year-old man in central Sweden who told me about his grandmother, who was born in Västerbotten but who lived in Västerås until her death a few years ago at age eighty-five. She made felt socks for him to wear in his fishing boots. The grandson claims that there is no match for felt socks, especially in very cold weather.

The name for felt socks varies from province to province in Sweden. In Västerbotten they are called *tovesockar* (felt socks), in Jämtland, *ullsocker* (wool socks), and in Hälsingland, *tossen*.

Some wore shoes made from felt, particularly members of large families living under meager circumstances. Hard-felted shoes made suitable substitutes for expensive leather ones.

Felt shoes were made thicker and denser (fulled harder) than felt socks. They were usually undyed gray or white fleece, but some shoes were dyed blue for boys, red for girls, and black for adults. If a shoe was too wide, the top was sometimes cut and wrapped to the side and buttoned. If it was too narrow, it was cut and closed with laces. Some shoes were decorated with simple wool yarn embroidery or finished with a crocheted edge or trimmed with white rab-

bit fur. Shoes were strengthened with an extra sole of vadmal (heavily fulled woven cloth) or leather.

In the Ullångers district of Ångermanland, felted shoes were called *ullskor* (wool shoes), in Multrå in Ångermanland they were called *tofskor* (tuft shoes), in Hälsingland, *tösser*, and in Vilhelmina and Stensele in Västerbotten, *tussar* (wads).

Insoles

Felt insoles for ski boots and tall boots were evidently not common; at least, they are seldom mentioned. Nevertheless, felt insoles can be found in Hälsingland. They are strengthened with densely sewn stitches of cotton thread. An elderly woman in Västerbotten remembers them being called *bottenklutar* (bottom patches).

Mittens

Felt mittens were not as common as felt socks, presumably because the thumb was difficult to make. Some children's mittens were dyed and embellished with an edging of crochet or fringe around the wrists. Leather was sewn

Felt socks are often used inside short boots and ski boots.

onto the thumb grips of some felted mittens to strengthen them.

Hats

Home-crafted felt hats and caps were rare, perhaps because they were readily available from professional hatmakers in marketplaces and in towns. Katarina Ågren proposes that the use of the word *tovhatt* (felt hat) in an estate inventory from 1804 in the Lövånger district indicates that at least some home-crafted hats were made. She argues that professional hatmakers would not have used the dialect word *tova* to describe their products. The word *hattov* (felt hat) is included in a record from Häggenås in Jämtland.

The Rusksele homestead museum in Västerbotten houses two felt hats of different styles. Both were made by Östen Olofsson Sundberg (1811–1892). One hat has a low, round crown with a turned-up brim and is stiff. The other is softer and is shaped similar to a hunter's hat with the brim turned up in the back only. Both have a leather sweatband and hat band around the crown. The soft hat is lined with cotton sheeting. The hats were probably made of natural black wool that has faded to brown over the years.

During the 1850s in Multrå in Ångermanland, hats as well as shoes were made of felt, and are largely the result of a "hat man" having moved there and taught the technique.

At the turn of the century, both men's and women's hats were felted in Norsjö and Skellefteå. A tailor in Stensele made hats that were probably made exclusively for men, although women of the district wore hats sometime later.

During the 1920s, a woman in the Vilhelmina region made women's hats with round crowns and various brims. They were dyed and finished with rosettes and ribbons. When berets were fashionable in the 1940s in Burträsk, they were felted.

A boy who was raised in Västerbotten wore a soft little cap of white felt, trimmed with a cotton ribbon. Similar

Erika Ullmark in Kålsta, Ullånger, Ångermanland, pounds wool shoes to make them durable. On the bench are a wooden shoe last and a fulled shoe.

summer caps were likely to have been common in this region. Although we do not know exactly how the hats were made, a wooden hat block found in Vilhelmina tells us how they were shaped.

Felt practitioners

"Every woman can spin," is an old Swedish saying. But the same could not be said for felting. In most villages, only a couple of women knew the craft. Many complained that felting was heavy, hard work that caused the hands to ache, and few enjoyed working with their hands in water for hours at a time. Some housewives with large families made felt to provide their husbands and children with warm socks. Many women in need of extra money would travel to farms to make felted articles for the residents. Some of these women fully supported their families through felting.

In Svedjeholmen in the Själevad district of Ångermanland, a story is told about a poor family with ten children who, in the beginning of the 1900s, learned to felt from an old Lapp man who had traveled to the village. They kept the technique secret to increase their earnings from the craft. The mother carded the wool, and the father felted with the children's help. Eventually, knowledge of the technique leaked out, and Svedjeholmen became a center for a felt sock industry. The socks were sold by the gross.

Ågren also writes about the mechanization of felting. In Svedjeholmen, Valter Östman and his wife learned to felt according to the old Lapp man's method, but they soon hit upon the idea of building an apparatus that allowed a cream separator to be used for felting the fleece. The family moved to Bjärtrå in

1922 and established a wholesale carding business in 1939. They used their machine to card fleece for sock suppliers, and the business thrived despite widespread unemployment. Near the end of the Second World War, wool was difficult to obtain and production was interrupted. At this time, Östman designed and built a simple machine to improve the efficiency of the process, and when he resumed felting in 1946, the business grew to a small industry that produced 1,500 pairs of socks each year. After 1967, the factory operated sporadically and has now ceased operation.

In the beginning of the 1900s, felt sock contract work brought a higher price than knitted socks, although knitted socks took much longer to make. It took more wool for a pair of felt socks, and the materials cost more than the hourly wage. The lower value of knitted socks can also be ascribed to the fact that knitting was commonly done by women at home during their little spare time. Felted socks were more in demand than knitted ones, and this helped to give them a higher price.

Material and technique

Opinions differed about which wool and which techniques produced the best felt. Despite conflicting views, most felters agreed that the fleece must be soft and have a short, well-developed crimp. Many favored the shorter spring fleece; others preferred long fall fleece blended with finer fleece. Long wool, known as rya wool, is very strong and therefore appropriate for socks. Goat hair, dog hair, and horsehair were sometimes blended in. Black fleece was considered by all to have properties inferior to white; it was more difficult to felt and not as warm. However, black fleece was blended with white to make gray.

The fleece was usually prepared with a carding bench or hand carders, but many different methods were used for the rest of the felting process. Resist templates were made of cloth, wood, paper (which was removed before the fleece was soaked), and shoe lasts (wooden

Viola Asplund warms her equipment and fleece before bench-carding the wool. Photo taken in 1967.

forms around which shoes are shaped). Some people even felted shoes entirely without a template! Most felters used warm, soapy water, but some worked without soap, and some added salt. Felters spattered water onto the fleece with whisks, strainers, or even by spitting. A grooved wooden washboard was commonly used for fulling, but smooth boards were also used, such as those used in Själevad (the board was rubbed back and forth on top of fleece lying on a table). To make felt dense enough for shoes, the felt was then thumped with a wooden club on a chopping block.

Viola Asplund—felt sock master

Viola Asplund, born in 1916, lives in Nyliden, outside of Skellefteå, and is one of the women responsible for bringing traditional feltmaking to the twentieth century. Västerbotten Museum turned to her in 1966 to document the technique.

Viola learned to felt from her mother.

"When we came home from school we had to sit and card wool—this was the children's chore," she recounts. Feltmaking had been a necessity in all rural farm homes. The people wore felt socks inside low boots of somewhat thin and hard leather. But it wasn't until Viola married and became a farm wife that she began felting in earnest. "I needed to keep my husband in felt socks for his work boots, and felt was naturally easy to maintain and was warm." Viola's four children would run in and out of the house in their felt socks. Dense felt was a necessity if the socks were to hold up.

The socks that Viola felted for her husband would, as a rule, last one year. The best wool for the socks was Lantras (an indigenous sheep) wool blended with both guard hair and down wool. Pure Rya (long wool) or pure Swedish Fin wool was not as good, according to Viola. People were also very careful to blend the different parts of a shorn fleece to one homogeneous quality. Viola also made socks for sale. In the 1940s and 1950s, many power stations were constructed, and Viola felted socks for the construction workers at a cost of two crowns (about forty cents) per pair.

Viola has taught the art of felting to her children and grandchildren, but it is she who furnishes them with the socks they need. "I felt a stockpile for the future, so that there are always some to take from," says Viola as she tells her grandchild to pull a pair of purchased cotton stockings over her felted socks before running outside in the crusty snow.

At nearly seventy-eight years old, Viola remains very active with her handwork. Most of all, she likes to sew bedspreads of fur pelts and to spin. "Felting is, of course, a little difficult," she says. She has placed her products in the Liljevalch art gallery in Stockholm. The Swedish Home-craft Society's National Association has given her a Gold Merit Award. When asked about what textile work has meant to her through the years, she laughed and said, "I have had so much fun!"

Norway

There are few historic records of felt manufacturing in Norway. Felt socks, called *ladder, labber* or *tövelabber,* were made at home in northern Norway. Felt socks with attached leather soles were worn when the weather was cold and dry. Felting was considered a very difficult job, but some farm wives felted socks for the money they would bring.

Felted socks were also sold in the markets, and some imported felt products were sold in commercial establishments in Finnmark. The *russekatankerna,* stiffened and hard-fulled felt high boots from the former Soviet Union, were highly regarded for wear outside the home.

Kirsten Julie Smådahl writes in her book, *Filting av Ull,* that Anna Grostøls reports evidence that felt socks called *dossa* were made in northern Norway. The word comes from the Finnish word for felt sock, *huopatossa.* In Namdalen, felt socks with hard felt soles, called *namdalslabber,* were made.

Wool shoes from Nesna

In Korgen, south of Mo i Rana, sewn felt shoes have been made as a cottage industry since the 1950s. The shoes resemble ordinary low boots with ties, and remain popular today. In Nesna, which lies outside Mo i Rana, a center was established (New Nesna Factory, Inc.) where the materials could be ordered, and the pieces cut and sent out to women in the district to be sewn together into shoes. The felt is commercially made in Halmstad. Today, district women still sew felt shoes in their own homes, but the soles and holes for shoelaces are added at the factory. In addition to the traditional Nesna *lobber,* felt shoes and slippers of a more modern style are also made. The various types of shoes and slippers are exported to the United States, Canada, and even to Sweden.

The classic Nesna *lobber* (felt shoes).

Wool shoes from Haus.

Wool shoes from Haus

Felt hats have long been a specialty of several farms in Osterøj and have been worn by both men and women of the area. Maria Hermundsdal, a specialist in hat felting, experimented with wool shoes in her old age. Maria received an order for a pair of wool shoes from an elderly man who wanted shoes as warm as her felted hats. The shoes were so successful that Maria taught another woman to make them, and thus the technique spread through the village.

Gradually, the production was organized. Just outside of Bergen, in the town of Haus, the Haus Self-help Office opened a wool processing plant in 1911. Fleece was carded at the plant and then sent on to the townswomen to make into felt shoes. At the peak of production, forty households with a total of 100 persons were employed in the manufacture of wool shoes. Entire families worked together, and although it was a subsidiary occupation for most, it provided the sole income for some households—especially during and after the Second World War, when requests for shoes were numerous. Even today, wool shoes can be purchased from Haus.

During the Second World War, felting underwent a renaissance in the countryside. Shortages of all types of goods necessitated that all available materials be used in all ways possible. Old felt hats were commonly cut up to make the soles of new wool shoes.

Maria Hermundsal (1815–1908), who developed the Haus felt shoes.

Finland

In northern and eastern Finland, felting was also practiced as a home craft. After the Second World War, the felting tradition began to fade in the north. In eastern Finland, the craft essentially stopped in the 1960s, but during the 1980s, Katarina Ågren's book inspired renewed interest.

During the Russian period (1809–1917), several factories were established in Finland to manufacture felt boots and socks, which helps to explain why felting does not exist as a home-craft in the southern part of the country. The first factory was started in Kirvu in 1897, and was soon followed by others, all established with Russian technology. The early steps of weighing the fleece and sewing the fleece around the templates of felt boots were done by hand, however. Production declined during the Second World War, largely as a result of material shortages.

There are presently five felt factories in Finland, two of which (Alhon Huopatehdas and Lahtisen Huopatehdas) manufacture boots and socks. Both factories are in Jämsä.

Commercially manufactured felt socks and boots are traditional winter footwear in Finland. Felt socks are still worn in the house or inside boots and are part of the Finnish army's winter apparel. Loggers and farmers wear felt socks for all outdoor activities, including haying. Children commonly wear felt boots, some of which have rubber glued onto the soles to make them wearable during the mud season. Felt boots are warmer than leather boots and cost about the same.

Felt socks and boots produced in Finland are exported to Canada, Sweden, and Germany, among other countries. Both have been modified for high-fashion use. While the classic boots are usually gray or brown, many clothing designers have used the traditional shapes in new colors. Contemporary children's boots are commonly blue and red.

The term *huopatossut* refers to both felt boots and socks, while *huopasylingit* or just *sylingit* refers only to felt socks. *Huopa,* which means "felt", is an Old Norse word. Swedish-speaking Finns call felt socks *filttossor* or *sylingar.*

BELOW: Felt boots *(huopatossut), sylingar (sylingit),* and other felt products from Koskenpään Huopatehdas in Jämsä.
BELOW LEFT: Antti Parviainen, Säyneinen, Kaavi, in felt boots with extra soles, 1908. Museum of Industry, Finland.

Felting Techniques in Other Cultures

Feltmaking in Mongolia

In the fourth century B.C., the Chinese referred to the large Central Asian steppes as "the land of felt". Felt still plays an important role in the lives of the nomads who continue to tend livestock as their main source of livelihood. The Mongolian livestock tenders in mountainous regions traveled seasonally between pastures, from winter pastures in the valleys to spring and fall pastures halfway up the mountains and summer pastures high in the mountains. A network of roads as we know them didn't exist, and they had only camels and horses to transport themselves and their goods. Consequently, they traveled lightly, taking only the necessary furnishings. Their large flocks of sheep produced, and in a sense actually transported, food as well as material for tents, carpets, clothing, dung for fuel, and ankle bones used for the children's game *shagai*.

Felt is especially well suited for nomadic life because it utilizes the sheep on hand, requires only simple equipment, and can be executed in a short, albeit intense, period of time. The quality and thickness of the felt can be varied to suit different needs; from thick, windproof felt for tents to thin, flexible felt for stockings.

Although industry is responsible for most of the production, felt is still made as a handicraft in Mongolia. When I was in Mongolia in 1991, I learned that the people in the district around Ulan Bator had stopped making felt as a handicraft and that all of the local wool was sent to factories or exported. After the downfall of the socialist system in 1990, the people had obtained a large amount of freedom and the individual villages were able, to a great extent, decide for themselves what would be done with their wool.

The political changes have brought about an interest in ancient Mongolian history. Genghis Khan is once again a

Zachas in Manhan, Northwestern Mongolia, make felt with the help of a camel.

folk hero, and the old Mongolian writing has been reintroduced as the official script. Interest in old traditions, including feltmaking, has flourished. Although the school curriculum does not yet include the culturally important feltmaking techniques, there is hope that it will.

During the socialist period (1923–1990), knowledge of feltmaking was held by the nomadic tribal minorities who continued to tend livestock in the distant regions of northwest Mongolia.

Before the introduction of Communism in 1932, relatives and close neighbors assembled to make felt; afterward felt was made in village collectives. Men and women worked together, and large pieces of felt were always a group effort; it was too heavy and difficult for one person to manage, and working in a group helped the task go more quickly. The collective work also provided the opportunity for a festival! The Mongolians don't believe in a life consisting exclusively of

In Mongolia there are sheep breeds both with fat tails and with short tails. The fat-tailed type, shown here, have tails of medium length. The tail was once used by Mongolians for food for a journey—it is regarded a delicacy! The character of the wool varies somewhat. The fleece contains both a fine-fibered undercoat and coarse guard hair, and the staple has large waves. Lamb fleeces can be very soft, and are used by the Mongolians for the finest felt.

work; all collective work is ended with hours of food, drink, and song.

Felt, *esgij,* is usually made during the period from the end of August to the beginning of September, after the sheep's second and final shearing of the year. Small items such as boots can be made during other times of the year, but large felt pieces are made outdoors in the late summer.

The wool that is shorn in the fall is preferred for felt. Travelers to Mongolia hold different opinions on the quality of the spring wool clip versus the fall wool clip. Some assert that the spring wool is longer and finer. Sheer logic says that this cannot be so, because it is in the summer that the sheep have access to better pasture, which improves their fleece. Spring wool may be considered finer because the down wool is combed with a special wool comb used to separate the guard hair from the down wool. Down wool is naturally finer and softer than the fall wool, which is composed of the whole fleece.

The process of making felt

One hot day at the end of August, I attended a feltmaking session outside of Ulan Bator with an extended family of Chalcha Mongolians. They had not made felt for many years, but an old woman among them had retained the knowledge and led the work. I had seen feltmaking at a collective in Manhan in northwest Mongolia, and have discovered that the process varies somewhat between different folk groups, although the principles are the same. The photographic descriptions that follow are from these two feltmaking sessions and are presented to show the differences.

Felt festivals

Ceremonies surrounding feltmaking are important. At the feltmaking session mentioned above, the old feltmaker blessed the felt by using an offering staff, *tatchjal,* to sprinkle fermented mare's milk, *ajrag,* to all four points of the compass before the felt roll was opened on the steppe.

1. Before feltmaking, the wool is beaten with sticks by two or three people. The sticks used by the Chalcha Mongolians are approximately 1 meter (39 inches) long and made of willow, a flexible wood. Some of the Zachas use iron rods instead. The black iron warms in the sun and therefore softens the lanolin in the wool. The ends of the iron rods are wrapped with wool to make them more comfortable to hold.

The fiber is beaten along the line of the fiber, which separates the wool fibers and helps to remove dirt trapped between them. This gives a coarser result than carding. The top of the fibers point both upward and downward, making it possible for them to grip onto the wool layers that will be put on top of them.

2. An old felt, called the "mother felt" is rolled out onto the field.

It is traditional to sit in a circle around a beautiful ceremonial felt carpet and drink a prosperity toast before felting begins. The host bids for luck and leads all of those present with a bowl of ajrag. Always handed from right hand to right hand, the bowl is first filled for the most honored guest and then is given back to the host, who fills it again,

leather are put over the two ends of the pole. The ends of the poles used by the Zachas have wooden eyelets or wooden pieces with drilled-out holes.

3. The stick-beaten wool is placed on the mother felt following a special technique. A good-sized tuft of beaten wool is taken in the right hand and laid down on the mother felt. The left hand is then placed on the wool hanging out of the right hand and is pressed down onto the mother felt. The right hand, with some wool still in it, is then pulled out. A tuft of wool is thus left behind on the mother felt with the fibers somewhat parallel to the other tufts.

5. After all the layers are laid out (the number of layers dictated by the desired thickness), the wetting of the wool begins. Warm water is poured over an outstretched hand that causes it to splash out in small drops over the wool. I did not see that any soap was added to the water. Other sources (Gösta Montell and A. Róna-Tas), also make no mention of soap or other fulling solution being used by Mongolian feltmakers. Prewashing away the wool's fatty acids and potassium salts evidently serves the same function as using soap.

A large, sturdy pole, with a diameter of about 10 to 12 cm (4 to 4³/₄ in), is placed on one end of the laid-out wool, and both mother felt and laid-out wool are rolled tightly around it.

7. From the loops, a rope about 40 meters (43 yards) long is tied to two horses or one camel. Then the felt is drawn over the steppe. The horsemen ride; the camelman leads his animal.

After a few hours, the felt roll is unwrapped and the felt examined by the feltmaking leader. In this case, a few weak places were found and promptly strengthened with fiber cut from the tail of a horse. The tail hairs were cut into short pieces, laid on the weak spots, covered with bits of wool, sprinkled with water, and covered with small pieces of cloth. Then the mother wool and fleece were rolled up again.

4. The best and whitest wool is laid out first and establishes the right side of the felt. Unwashed, uncarded (unbeaten) whole fleeces are used in the middle layer. The more lanolin in this wool, the better; it speeds the felting process. The inferior wool, coarse and brown, is placed on top and will become the back side of the felt.

6. Wet hides are wound around the felt roll. Soaking the hides strengthens and softens them—dry hides would break apart during the vigorous rolling action. Strong rope is wrapped around the roll, and loops of

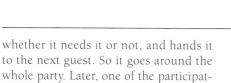

whether it needs it or not, and hands it to the next guest. So it goes around the whole party. Later, one of the participating men reads good wishes, called *jörööl*, over the felt.

Because we had to get on the road as soon as the feltmaking ended and could

not stay for the traditional party, we attended a similar party the previous evening. For the occasion, a sheep was slaughtered, the liver was grilled over an open fire, the intestines were made into sausage casing, and the meat pieces were surrounded with onions and red-hot

stones in a large milk can, which was shaken vigorously. Ajrag and vodka made from milk, *archi*, were served continually from a beautiful silver bowl, and the Mongolians sang songs all evening. This, I am told, is a proper felt party!

Yurts—the nomad's home

Yurts, the nomads' classic tent made of a wooden framework covered with several thick layers of felt, can still be seen throughout Mongolia. Ulan Bator, the capital, with a population of 500,000, contains orderly neighborhoods made up exclusively of yurts in which people live year round. Outside Ulan Bator are summer camping areas of yurts occupied by city residents seeking to escape the hustle and bustle of modern city life. Yurts can even be found in the gardens of some high-rise apartment buildings.

For Mongolians, the yurt is the symbol of a free nomadic life. The English researcher Peter Andrews, Ph.D., has studied yurts for many years. Our word "yurt" is derived from the Turkish word describing the place where a tent stood. Today, in Turkey, the word refers to a student dormitory. The Mongolians call a felt tent a *ger,* and the Kirghiz use the term *öj*. In Mongolian, *ger* refers to the home and is used even when referring to other types of domiciles. However, the word "yurt" is used so often in the Western world that I will use it here, so as to avoid misunderstanding.

Peter Andrews believes that the Turks first made yurts without a wooden framework. He theorizes that the Kita or Uigur people (ancient Turks who spread across Asia by the fifth century) introduced the yurt to the Mongolians in the ninth century. The Mongolians have since made numerous variations of this perfect nomad home. The yurt has been used by most of the nomadic people of Central Asia in somewhat different executions but similar principles. The different forms most likely came about in response to different climatic conditions. In Kyrgyzstan, for example, where there is an abundance of rainfall, the yurt's roof is high and steep. In Mongolia, where strong winds are common, the crown of the yurt is held up with a roof pole.

Today, both wooden frameworks and the felt covers are available ready-made from yurt factories in Mongolia. These yurts are made according to government standards and are built in the traditional manner. However, the tradition of handwork has endured among the resident minority groups. Yurts made by the Kazakhs in northwest Mongolia have a different form from those made by the largest minority group, the Chalcha. The Kazakhs continue to make their yurt frames by hand.

In his novel *Farväl Gulsary,* the Kirghiz author Tjingiz Ajtmatov writes how the state's issuing clerks decided that for economic reasons synthetic material would replace wool felt for yurt coverings. The result was that people nearly froze to death during the winter and sweltered in the summer. The bureaucrats in this novel didn't know about wool's unique insulating properties against both cold and heat, a characteristic that is essential for survival on the high plateaus where temperature range is extreme. The temperature inside a wool yurt is even and comfortable, and the atmosphere is special; the circular form creates harmony and presence, the felt walls, a feeling of warmth, and the height, a sense of open spaciousness. The smoke hole, a wooden ring that sits across the middle of the roof, is usually open; it is covered only during rain or cold. It wonderful to sleep wrapped in felt rugs in this warm, soft room, to look at the stars through the smoke hole, and to hear the night sounds from the steppe outside.

The smoke hole in a modern yurt accommodates the chimney pipe of a simple sheet-metal stove used to provide warmth and heat for cooking. In earlier times, the smoke hole provided an escape route for the smoke from an open fireplace in the center of the yurt. Some of the smoke would filter through the felt roof, and the resulting buildup of smoke particles would make the felt resistant to rain. But with time, the smoke also made the felt brittle. Many yurts have fitted covers of strong white cotton or hemp for protection. The cover also makes the yurt white, a color that has traditionally been an indication of affluence. The smoke from the open fires would turn

Zachasjin yurt. The size of the yurt varies according to function and tribal group. Most yurts have six to nine wall sections and are 5 to 6 meters (16½ to 19¾ feet) wide. Heights can reach 2.5 meters (8 feet) or more. Festival and guest yurts can be somewhat larger, while yurts used for traveling to the pasture areas tend to be smaller.

A Zachasjin yurt is raised in Manhan, northwestern Mongolia, 1991. The roof is lifted after the wall segments have been put into place.

Roof ribs are stuck into holes in the crown ring and are bound tightly to the ribs in the wall segments.

the felt brownish black quickly. An affluent person could change the yurt's felt often, thereby maintaining a clean, white home. White is still a respected and appreciated color among the Mongolians, and it is used during ceremonies and feasts.

Wooden framework

The yurt consists of an ingenious wooden skeleton with a number of wall sections made of latticework. The lattice pieces are made of cross-laid ribs, which can be pushed together like an accordion when the time comes to move the yurt. The wall sections and door frame are stood upright in a circle and wrapped together with woven bands or ropes of camel hair. No anchoring ropes are needed to support the strong and elastic walls. Though the steppe winds are strong, there are no straight sides to catch the wind—it is diverted around the circular yurt. Sven Hedin, an explorer and collector of Mongolian artifacts for the People's Ethnographic Museum in Stockholm, appreciated the ingenuity of the round yurt during one of his expedi-

The rope for tying the yurt's felt is either two flattened pieces of three-strand braid sewn together side by side or round braid plied together.

tions into Central Asia, when his four-sided British military tent was blown down.

After the walls are put into place, the crown ring, with its cross of six arches, is held up with one or two supporting bars. The Kazakhs use two bars, while other Mongol tribes use only one. The roof sticks are thrust into holes in the crown ring and then are securely attached to the ribs in the latticework with camel-hair lacing that is tightly knotted to the roof ribs' ends. With a simple hand movement, they are wrapped high up around the ribs' cross.

Afterward, a wide woven band is knotted around the middle of the walls from door jamb to door jamb, and two large felt pieces are wrapped around the yurt and tightly knotted to the wood framework. The shaped roof felt is then laid onto the roof ribs. To finish, rope is knotted on top of the felt.

Manufacturing the yurt's wooden frame

When I was with a Torgut family in the Altai in northwest Mongolia, I had a chance to see how a piece of the yurt's wooden section was manufactured. The Torgut are an ancient people who live remotely and have kept to traditional methods. They also have access to the much-needed willow, which grows in groves by the river Bulgan.

1. The bark of green willow branches is peeled with a simple knife. The branches are then steamed into soft S-shapes to be used as the wall ribs. The ribs are warmed in a long sheet-iron oven and then bent between sticks in the workbench.

2. Among the Torgut, the ribs are painted with a red earth pigment that is dissolved in water. The ribs are fastened together with leather bits, which are pulled through holes in the sticks.

3. To make the holes, the men use a very simple and ingenious drill that is driven by a cord. A nail in each end of the drill makes it possible to drill holes in two ribs at the same time.

4. Many Mongolian tribal groups have wooden doors on their yurts. These are commonly decorated with painted patterns. The threshold is part of the door frame and is very high, perhaps to keep the goats and sheep from entering the yurt. It is considered a very serious breach of etiquette to tread on a door's threshold.

The interior of a Torgut yurt from Etsin-Gol, Inner Mongolia, in the 1930s. Opposite the door, which faces south, is the master's place. Before the introduction of socialism, there was an altar on the north wall. Male guests were placed on the host's right side, while women sat to his left. From the roof hang tufts of fleece from animals that had been sold.

The Peoples Ethnographic Museum, Stockholm, from which this photograph comes, have two Mongolian yurts with fittings collected by Sven Hedin. One of them is a unique temple yurt.

The wooden doors of Zachasjin yurts are covered with a quilted felt that can be rolled up and down. Two quilted shou symbols decorate the one shown here.

Sewn Felt Carpets in Mongolia

Carpets are an important interior decoration that commonly cover the entire floor of a Mongolian's yurt or house. They are used to sit and sleep on and may be used as a table. The Kazakhs in northwest Mongolia pile them high on their beds as a sign of prosperity.

The traditional, entirely handmade carpets are still used, even though factory-made carpets of various types are available for purchase. Carpets of machine-made felt are machine quilted with cotton thread and are not as durable as handmade ones. A handmade carpet is likely to last at least twenty years.

As with wool for yurts, material for carpets is also scarce. Most of the wool is reserved for industrial use or exported. It is therefore among the nomadic minority groups, where the traditional lifestyle still exists, that handmade carpets are made in the old way.

The techniques used to ornament and decorate the carpets made today are identical to those used in the grave discoveries from Pazyryk and Noin Ula.

Different minority groups in Mongolia have managed this inheritance in different ways. The Kazakhs are known for their lively patterned carpets called *syrmak*, while other groups use the wool's natural white color to make carpets with more conservative designs.

According to Ottó Farkas, a Hungarian researcher studying the Mongolian people, the Kazakh word *syrmak* or *syrdak* and the Mongolian name for felt carpet, *shirdeg*, all come from the root *syr* or *shir*, meaning "to quilt". All the Mongolian carpets are densely quilted. Most often the quilting stitches are worked on white felt, and the design is built through the quilting lines. The Kazakhs' multicolored *syrmak* carpets are worked with mosaic and appliqué, but finished with quilting.

Monochromatic carpets with quilting—shirdeg

The most common type of felt carpet in Mongolia is monochromatic with the entire surface covered in dense quilting. To call the carpets monochromatic is perhaps misleading; many have a small edge border or decoration in a contrasting color. But the background color is the natural white of the wool.

Chalcha Mongolians put a small red border on the edge of their carpets. The

Grandparents with their grandchildren on a colored *syrmak* carpet in the Kazakh summer pasture in the Altai mountains.

Torgut and Zachas carpets commonly have linear motifs decorating the four corners and a linear border around the entire carpet, all in lustrous black goat wool.

Both spring and fall wool is used for carpets. The thicker spring wool is used for the under layer, while the softer fall wool becomes the upper layer. The wool in the under layer is often light brown. Many sheep in Mongolia have a color that resembles light camel fiber. Brown wool is used for the under layer because it is considered to be less valuable than white wool. To make the wool whiter still, the Chalcha Mongolians bleach it with bone ash. The carpets can also be made of two separate felts, one white and one light brown, and the two layers quilted together.

The making of carpet felt

In 1991, I watched a Torgut Family in Bulgan make a felt carpet.

Torgut carpet felt is made exclusively by hand by women. The wool is beaten with a stick in the same way that tent wool is prepared (see page 24). The wool is laid out the same way on a mat that is woven from a rigid steppe grass called *tjii* (also known as *chij* or *chi*). The wool is sprinkled with warm water and the mat is rolled up. Rope is laid in loops around the mat, and the ends are threaded through the loops. The mat roll is then rotated by three or four women using their forearms. When the wool is felted, they remove the felt and roll it for a little while without the mat. More water is poured over the rolled felt as needed during the course of the work.

The quilting

When the felt is fulled and dry, the quilting begins. Traditionally, the linear pattern was marked with earth pigments. Many now use synthetic dyestuff. In either case, the marking disappears with use. Quilting, like felting, is done by a group of several women who all sew on the same carpet. This collective work is, in essence, a quilting bee. The only difference is that the Mongolians do not use a batting—it isn't needed with the stiff felt.

The quilting thread is a strong two-ply thread of undyed camel hair that has been spun on a spindle. Sheep wool is not used because wool thread can shrink and break. A felt carpet can be up to 2 centimeters (1 inch) thick, so the needle is stuck straight down through the layers to get a fine linear pattern. The right side faces upward while the carpet is stitched so that the stitches on the right side will be straight (those on the back can be somewhat lopsided). A simple running stitch is used, which in the finished carpets forms small dots. On a Torgut carpet, the stitches are about 2 millimeters (less than 1/8 inch) long and there are fifteen to seventeen stitches to 10 centimeters (4 inches). The distance between the quilting lines can be 1.5 to 2 centimeters (3/4 to 1 inch). The carpet is quilted from the middle out to the edge. It is heavy work to pull the large, sharp

needle through the felt and to draw up the stitches—the stitches must be drawn so hard that the quilting sinks down into the felt and creates a pretty line. Because the thread is sunken into the felt, it is not exposed to wear.

Composition and ornament

The quilting performs both an aesthetic and practical function. The monochromatic surface is made pretty by the contrast between light and shadow, and the felt is made more permanent and durable because the stitches hold it together. In quilted carpets, the pattern is made exclusively from the closely packed quilting lines. The entire surface is filled with evenly spaced lines.

The lines form a pattern consisting of a border around a center field. The center field can be filled with the ancient spiral shapes known from the Noin Ula discoveries. The field can also be divided into three or four smaller quadrangles, each filled with different patterns.

One of the most popular patterns is a variation of the Chinese *shou* motif. Even in today's Chinese textiles, the shou is used repetitively as a fill-in pattern. Chinese silk is commonly used in Mongolian clothing, and another popular pattern, which occurs in many variations, is the "endless knot". It is one of the eight symbolic offerings in the lamaistic iconographs and has broad artistic usage in

Several Torgut women help to quilt a carpet. The motif that stands out so clearly is sewn in black yarn made of goat hair.

both Mongolia and Tibet. This motif symbolizes long life and prosperity. Heart shapes and triangles are also used in the center field.

The patterns used in these carpets are nonfigurative. They have different sources and can be symbolic. The Mongolians manipulate the patterns in ways that are specific to them. The absence of human and animal images on everyday objects is linked to lamaistic ideas. In Central Asia, images held a magic function. They were used in shamanistic seances, and their potential power was not to be invoked frivolously.

Edge, border and linear ornament

The black border of lacing sewn over the quilting along the carpet's edge is both aesthetic and practical. It strengthens the edge and holds the carpet together. The border does not cover the cut, felt edge, but overlies the felt 1 to 2 centimeters (1/2 to 1 inch) in from the edge. In some Torgut carpets, there are two yarns sewn to the carpet side by side. One yarn

is spun with an S twist, the other with a Z twist. The material is shiny black goat hair chosen from only the longest fibers of the fleece. The goat hair is spun and plied tightly into a strong two-ply yarn. The needle is stuck through the felt layer and through one yarn, drawn through, and then stuck through the other yarn and back down through the felt layer. When the stitch is drawn up, the thread does not show in the yarn on the face. The stitches repeat with perhaps a 1-centimeter (1/2-inch) gap. The finished width of the border is about 1.2 centimeters (5/8 inch).

The same black shiny yarn is used for the occasional ornamental design placed in the corners or in the center of the carpet.

Felt carpets with mosaic patchwork—syrmak

The most complicated patterns and techniques are in the Kazakhs' *syrmak* carpets. The same technique, although with smaller pattern shapes and many more colors, is also used by the Kirghiz in their *shirdak* carpets.

The pattern is built from felt pieces that are connected together edge to edge,

At one time, even storage vessels were worked with strengthening and decorative quilting. This small lidded felt box was used to store a Mongolian's very important drinking bowl of silver and wood. Collection of the National Museum, Ulan Bator.

in a technique called encrustation, mosaic patchwork, or intarsia embroidery. In this technique, the join between pattern pieces is concealed with a couched yarn of a contrasting color, a technique that enhances the composition. In addition to mosaic patchwork, appliqué is used; another fabric is sewn on top of the felt as decoration. The prefix *syr* or *shir* in the name of the carpet technique indicates the importance of quilting. The entire surfaces of these carpets are covered with stitching, just as are those of

BELOW: Two women display a traditional Kazakh syrmak carpet of mosaic patchwork. The natural color of the wool is enlivened with red couching between the pattern shapes.

ABOVE: Running dog, wave, and spiral patterns are commonly used in borders. A double border with variations of the running dog can also be found. The border is the same width on all sides of the carpet.

the monochromatic carpets made by the Torgut and Chalcha Mongolians. The quilting stitches follow the pattern shapes.

Composition

The oldest syrmak carpets were made in two colors; natural black and natural white wool. Today, natural dyes and even synthetic dyes are used. The carpets are no longer limited to two colors, but often have three or four. They are dyed after the wool has been felted.

The classic composition of a syrmak has one center field, small borders on the long sides, and wider borders on the short sides. They are rectangular, often with the long sides twice the length of the short ones. A popular composition is of ram's horns with a border of running dogs. The pattern is worked in a positive/negative fashion; the same motifs are cut in two contrasting colors and used in opposite ways (the background from one color is exchanged for the background of the other). Small contrasting lines made by the couched colored threads between the pattern shapes give the composition more life.

1. **Mosaic Patchwork.** The first step in making a classic syrmak is to make three pieces of felt. One piece is made of each pattern color (white and black) from fine fall wool. The third piece, used for the back side, is made from inferior, coarse spring wool in a brownish color.

Positive and negative motifs are cut out of black and white felts with a sharp knife. The black pattern piece is laid into the opening in the white felt, and the white pattern piece into the opening in the black one. Then the pieces are sewn together with a two-ply

thread of camel hair with a simple overcast stitch. (An older method is to sew a simple zigzag stitch between the two pieces.)

The stitch is started from the underside, and with each stitch the thread crosses the edge of the felt. With this sewing technique, the edges don't overlap but lie side by side.

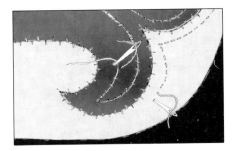

2. **Quilting stitch.** When the pattern pieces have been sewn together into a single solid surface, the surface is laid over the backing felt and sewn to it with quilting stitches. The stitches are made through both layers of felt, binding the layers together and forming a linear pattern on both the front and back of the carpet. The same technique is used for quilted monochromatic carpets (see page 30). The quilting can also be done as couching by laying a piece of yarn over the carpet and sewing it down with another yarn through the felt layers. The yarns can be of different colors.

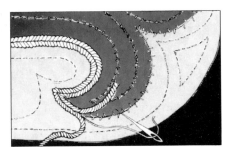

3. **Couching stitch.** The seams that connect the pattern pieces in the mosaic patchwork are then covered with a couched line of stitching, which the Kazakhs call *ziek*. This couched seam consists of two yarns, one with S twist and the other with Z twist. The couching stitch prevents the seams from splitting and at the same time is decorative. Couching is usually done after quilting.

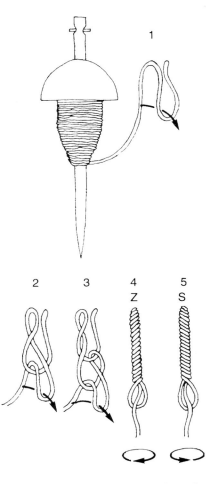

4. The direction of the twist depends on the direction in which the spindle is turned when spinning. The yarns are plied directly from the spindle by chaining some unwound yarn off in loops. The tension causes the yarn to twist itself to a tight cord. Using a singles yarn with a very tight twist, work a line of airy loops with the fingers. When the yarn is let go, the loops wind around themselves in the reverse direction. This creates a tight, three-ply yarn. When two yarns with opposite twists (one in the Z direction and one in the S direction) are sewn next to each other, a V effect is formed.

5. The yarns to be couched are sewn down so that the stitches joining them cannot be seen. The needle starts from the underside, goes through both felt layers and one of the yarns, and is pulled through. Then the needle is stuck through the other yarn and down through both felt layers. The stitches are placed about 1 cm (1/2 in) apart.

6. **Edge trim.** To strengthen the edge of the carpet, a trim of firmly-plied yarn is sewn 1 to 1.5 centimeters (1/2 to 3/4 inch) from the edge. This yarn can be made from horse, yak, or camel hair, or from sheep wool. This yarn is thicker than the yarn used over the mosaic patchwork, but it is spun and plied in the same way. The yarn is sewn on in pairs with S and Z twist to create a V effect. As many as three pairs of yarns can be used for a broader trim.

Appliqué

Besides mosaic patchwork, appliqué is also used in syrmak carpets. Traditionally, the appliqué was of thin felt, but today velvet, silk, and cotton cloth are used. The edges of appliqué motifs can be couched onto the felt with a single yarn or with a pair of S- and Z-twist yarns, just as seams are covered in mosaic patchwork. Appliqué is often worked in combination with mosaic patchwork. For example, the center field of a carpet may be sewn in mosaic patchwork and the border worked in appliqué.

Tambour Stitch in Kashmir

In Kashmir, the northernmost part of India, felt carpets and other objects of felt are decorated with tambour-stitch patterns. These carpets can sometimes be found in Indian import shops in Western countries. The carpets are known for their patterns of flowers and animal motifs. The residents of Kashmir call the embroidery "the poetry of handwork". Tea cozies, boots, and shepherd's mantles are also made of felt.

A pattern in tambour stitch commonly covers a large part of the felt's surface. As with the quilting in the Mongolian shirdeg carpets, the use of tambour stitch has the practical function of strengthening the felt. This is an important feature because the wool in Kashmiri carpets is blended with cotton to make it go further, and felt from such a blend is less durable than felt made exclusively of wool.

The wool-and-cotton blend is prepared with the carding bow. The bow is used both for opening up the fleece and cotton and for blending the fibers together.

The fiber blend is laid out on a reed mat, although the wool and cotton may be handled separately. In this case, cotton is laid between two layers of wool. Each layer is sprinkled with water and pressed down with a special tool before the next layer is added. The mat is rolled up, and

Tambour-stitch needle, *ari*, viewed from the top and side. It is similar to a sharp, flat crochet hook.

the felters begin to roll the mat under pressure with their feet. In the final stages, the mat is rolled by hand. After being washed, it is embroidered.

There are different ways to draw the pattern on the felt. Some workers use a wood printing block into which the pattern is carved and print with ink made from carbon. Some use the method that we know of as pouncing, a pattern of fine holes is punched in a durable fabric, and then a colored solution is pressed through these holes.

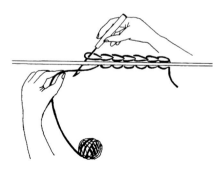

Tambour stitch. It is not easy to distinguish tambour stitch from chain stitch from the right side, but if you turn over the work, you'll see the difference. When the yarn is pulled through the felt in tambour stitch, a straight stitch is made on the back side. Chain stitch, on the other hand, makes disconnected uneven stitches on the back side because in such thick material, it is difficult to get a needle into the same hole twice.

Inlaid wool patterns in Turkmen carpets

In Mongolia today, two types of felt carpets are made: the quilted, monochromatic shirdeg carpet and the Kazakh syrmak, sewn in mosaic patchwork. The Turkmen also made a third variation, *keçe*. In making a keçe, colored wool is laid out in a pattern and felted into the carpet. We know this method as the inlaid technique.

Magnificent carpets with patterns of inlaid wool also exist in Kazakhstan and Kyrgyzstan. In Kazakh they are called *tekemet* and in Kirghiz, *alakiiz*.

The Turkmen people descended from Turks who emigrated from Mongolia in the tenth century. They live today in the southern part of the Turkmen Republic, formerly a part of the Soviet Union. Small groups live in northern Iran and Middle Asia.

István Vidák, a Hungarian felt researcher and artist, has studied feltmaking among the Turkmen, and he tells about their traditions.

The wool

The Turkmen shear their sheep twice each year. The fall wool, which is cleaner and shorter than the spring wool, is used for feltmaking. They use wool from Karakul and Szkarcsin breeds, both of which have wool of medium coarseness. The natural colors are gray, black, white, and brown. Traditionally, other colors were achieved by dyeing the wool with plant dyes, but today aniline dyes are used. The most common dyed colors are blue, red, and yellow. The wool is seldom washed, but it is always combed with a device made of a wooden plank with two rows of metal spikes.

Feltmaking

As a rule, four or five female relatives work together to make felt. Only women make carpets, and they make them for their own use.

Grid lines of loosely spun yarn are laid out on a straw mat to mark the edges of the pattern shapes. The pattern is then filled in with wool, and more wool is added for the backing. (The working side becomes the back.) The wool is sprinkled with water and the straw mat and wool are rolled together. Rope is wrapped around the roll and it is pulled back and forth with this rope.

After one hour, the mat is unrolled and then rolled again from the other end. After another hour of rolling back and forth, the roll is opened again, and thin places are layered with more wool and water. The felt is then rolled without the straw mat. The women get on their knees next to one another and roll the carpet with their forearms. This continues for another two to three hours, or until the carpet reaches the desired firmness. In the Turkmen tradition, felt is rolled twice each year to clean and freshen the carpets and remove any bad odors.

Felt carpets that are used as prayer rugs are made in the natural color of the wool and stay rolled up in a corner of the room when not in use.

Cut Felt Designs in Turkey

In Turkey, yet another type of patterned felt carpet is made. The pattern is cut out of loosely made felts in many colors and then is felted into the foundation wool.

Felt keçe are made by men in workshops. As many as three generations of a family may work together. The grandfather does the simpler tasks such as plucking apart the wool fleece and carding it. (A carding machine has replaced the ancient carding bow.) His son does the heavier work with the felt, and his grandson helps with the carding and the small tasks before and after school. The work is undertaken without conversation and at a fast pace. Felting machines have increased productivity: a workshop can now make seven or eight shepherd's mantles, *kepeneks,* in one day, but without the machines they could make only two in one day.

Laying out a Turkmen carpet at an international workshop in Kesckemét, Hungary.

The old method of making felt entirely by hand is carried on by just a few masters. In Konya, Mehmet Girgiç hand-felts the early stages of dervish hats and then works with his son to roll the felt. A man in Bergama continues to make carpets in the same way. There are even men in Urfa who full their felt by beating it against a large stone with their chests!

Felt production varies according to the needs of the inhabitants of a region. Most produce carpets, mantles, horse and donkey saddles, vests, and shoe soles. Beautifully embroidered prayer rugs are made for mosques. Among the nomads in the southern and eastern sections of the country, felt is used to strengthen bags and head ornaments for horses and camels. In addition to sheep wool, mohair, called *tiftik,* is used from domestic Angora goats.

Important centers for felt are Tire, Konya, Afyon, and Balikesir, but felt workshops also exist in many other places.

Head ornaments for a horse. Kurdish work. The triangles are of dark indigo-dyed felt and are richly decorated with shells, buttons, pieces of metal, and small glass beads. Tablet-woven bands and tassels complete the ornament.

Aristocracy among the Turkmen people is in part determined by the number of felted carpets owned. The patterns are beautifully and painstakingly laid out. The carpets may have patterns on both the front and back sides. The ram's horn is the most common motif, and it may fill the entire surface of a carpet with a soft and graceful design. The head motif in carpets from Ogulsirin is called *gotsch*. The borders around the carpets are about 20 centimeters (8 inches) wide.

One family may have fifty to sixty carpets. In the 1980s, a family would make five to six new carpets per year, but today woven carpets are more common.

Carpet made by Nuri Kömürcü in Kula, Turkey. The pattern has a certain local distinction but could have come from a number of different workshops in the same area. A large part of a day's felt production is managed as commission work. Peasants supply their own wool for a carpet or mantle to be made at a workshop.

1. The patterns are often elegant and intricate. The thin, softly felted pattern felt is cut into strips that are laid out on a rush mat. The workers pace off the middle of the mat and then lay out the pattern by eye. Undyed wool is then shaken over the pattern with easy motions using a special tool called a *cubuk*.

2. The wool is sprinkled with hot, soapy water, and the carpet is quickly rolled up inside the rush mat.

The first part of the felting, the stamping, is most often done by machine. After the roll is stamped, it is laid on the floor and opened up.

4. More wool is spread over the back side of the carpet using the *cubuk*. The last part of the process is done in another type of felt machine. Some machines are equipped with a small steam pan that forces hot steam into the felt. After washing, the carpet is beaten to strengthen it and set upright or hung to dry. A finished carpet is 1 to 2 centimeters (1/2 to 1 inch) thick.

Cubuk. A cubuk is made from about five peeled twigs knotted together with string or a leather strap. The twigs are threaded through holes in a piece of wood that holds them in a radiating position. The string is threaded between the bound area and the wood support several times to hold the twigs in place.

3. The edge is folded to the back and the fibers in the folded edge are twisted together with the fibers from the back side. The felt is crimped neatly at the corners like the edges of a meat pie.

These photos are from Kemal Erkus's workshop in Afyon and Cani Karayazgun's in Tire.

· 36 ·

Choosing Wool and Washing, Dyeing, and Carding

Wool Selection— The Most Important Factor

Is there anthing more thrilling than opening a sack of wool? To pull out the fleece and see the beautiful sheen and color! What luck, to hit upon a perfect Swedish Fin wool fleece with small crimp, shiny white color, and clean as well! Experience a bag of Pälsull (Gotland wool) with all its subtle gray tones from black to white. Come upon a Rya lamb fleece in which the ends of the long, silky locks have been bleached by the sun. Perhaps it is just such rich variations that make working wool so thrilling. Every sheep has a unique personality, as does its wool.

Nordic wool has all the qualities that a versatile feltmaker could wish for. The many variations in Nordic Short-Tail sheep accommodate all of the feltmaker's aesthetic and functional needs, and the wool felts exceptionally well. An American feltmaker uses Swedish Pälsull when she is in a hurry because it felts so quickly, while a Hungarian feltmaker complains that Swedish wool is too aggressive.

In all handwork, the material is as important as the design and technique— all three must be considered equally. Otherwise, the finished product may lack important qualities. For example, a beautifully designed and felted jacket is of little value if it feels too prickly to be worn comfortably.

The problem facing a feltmaker is that there is no consistent value, quality, or measurement for felting wool. A weaver can purchase a particular yarn and be confident that the yarn will have a predictable thickness, spinning quality, and fiber blend. However, what are you getting when you purchase Swedish Fin fleece or dyed roving? Purchased fleece may vary in coarseness and be blended with wool from a breed raised for meat, which would make the wool difficult to felt and the finished felt less durable. You can minimize this problem by learning as much as you can about wool and using only dependable suppliers.

Evaluating wool

Although you can get information about wool from sheep breeders and carding companies, to successfully evaluate wool you must learn how to see, smell, and feel the wool yourself.

Many inexperienced feltmakers make poor choices when selecting wool. When I was a novice feltmaker, I used wool received as a gift to make socks. Imagine my astonishment—and despair—when the wool would not felt. Upon close examination of the wool, I noticed that it was lusterless, spongy, tough, and rubbery; and although it had enough elasticity to be pressed into a small ball in my hand, as soon as I opened my hand, it instantly returned to its initial volume. It turned out that the wool came from a Texel sheep, a breed raised largely for meat.

After this adventure, I understood that it is important to look closely at a fleece, to examine the fiber length, thickness, luster, and crimp as well as the lock formation and structure. A common problem with Swedish wool is that it no longer comes entirely from purebred *Lantrasfår* (similar to Finnish Landrace) sheep. It has become common for these

---

Wool Equivalents

Many of the wool types mentioned in this book are not available in the United States. The following substitutions can be made.

Swedish Fin = Merino, Polwarth, Cormo, Rambouillet, Finn (Finnish Landrace)
Swedish Fin of Gobelin type = Corriedale, NZ halfbreed
Päls (Gotland) = (however, none of these wools felt as quickly or as nicely as the Gotland wool.) Romney, Coopworth, Leicester, Perendale (Gotland is imported to North America by Norsk Fjord Fiber)
Rya/Spelsau = Lincoln, Karakul, Churro, Icelandic (Spelsau is imported to North America by Norsk Fjord Fiber. Icelandic is imported to North America by Louise Heite.)

sheep to be crossed with meat breads to make them larger for butchering (for example, prolific Swedish Fin ewes crossed with large Texel rams). This crossbreeding affects the wool: felting with it takes longer and the resulting felt is spongy, thick, and not very durable. Depending on the way it's used, however, sponginess can be an advantage, which I will discuss later. It is important to know how to evaluate fleece and to understand how different fibers behave in different contexts.

Composition of wool fibers

Most sheep in Sweden come from the double-coated, Nordic Short-Tail family and have two distinct coats of wool.

The *undercoat* is comprised of fine, soft fibers that have a well-defined crimp. The scales of the fibers tend to overlap one another like the shingles on a roof, which minimizes the luster of the wool. The small diameter of the fiber causes it to reflect light poorly, which makes it look dull. Undercoat fibers absorb water easily.

The *outercoat* fibers are long, coarse, strong, elastic, and have little crimp. The scales of the fibers are large and lie edge to edge on the same plane, which gives the outercoat a high luster. These fibers are medullated (have a center of air-filled cells) and resist water.

The outercoat also contains *kemp*, short, medullated fibers. Kemp is brittle, coarse, and straight or only slightly wavy. It has no luster and is difficult to dye.

The fleece of older sheep breeds indigenous to Sweden, such as the Gute sheep, may contain all three hair types. The crimp in the undercoat captures air and is therefore warmer. The outercoat protects the undercoat from getting wet. The kemp hair helps spread the fleece so that it doesn't pack down.

A *staple* or *lock* is a group of fibers growing next to one another which are connected by their crimp to give the fleece a wavy appearance.

Undercoat

Outercoat

Kemp

Staple from a Rya fleece with a lamb lock at the tip. The small, curly lock does not reappear after the firsh shearing.

Recognizing good felting wool

If the wool is lustrous and forms distinct staples that are crimpy to wavy, it is likely a true *Lantrasull* and will have good felting qualities. The best wool for felting lacks the elasticity of fleece from meat sheep; that is, it won't pop back into its original shape after being squeezed in your hand. English Leicester wool, which has distinct staples and good luster, also felts easily. Leicester is a medium-coarse wool, and the breed is the result of crosses between many older English breeds.

A staple of Landrace fleece tapers into points and is made up of both outercoat and undercoat fibers. To separate the two fiber types, hold the tip of the staple in your right hand and the cut end in your left, and gently pull your hands apart. The outercoat will stay in your right hand and the undercoat in your left. In some cases, the differences between the two types are very small, as in wool from Swedish Fin sheep. In certain sheep breeds, such as the Texel, their outercoat is similar to the undercoat in terms of fineness and length. In others, such as the Leicester Longwool and Gotland, the undercoat is long and coarse and similar to the outercoat in appearance and characteristics.

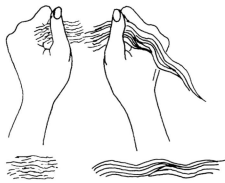

The undercoat and outercoat of Rya wool can easily be separated by hand.

Wool from heavy meat sheep

If the wool is white, lusterless, has no distinct staple structure, and appears spongy, it is probably from a meat breed. If you were to try to draw a lock of the fleece apart in your hands, you'd find little difference between the undercoat and outercoat fibers. The fibers may all be the same length and thickness, they will have small aberrations in crimp, and every fiber will stand alone. The fleece may appear as if it has already been carded. Wool from meat sheep breeds is very elastic: it will spring back quickly after being clamped down in your hand. The wool is difficult to felt by hand but can be mechanically fulled in woven cloth. This type of fleece is appropriate for use as an isolated middle layer of fiber or as stuffing fiber.

Sheep bred for meat production are easy to recognize. Because all of their fiber is usually the same length, their coats appear smooth, not pointed or shaggy.

In Sweden, there are six imported meat breeds. Besides the previously named Leicester, which does felt, several down breeds are imported from England. These are the Oxford, Shropshire, and Suffolk. Wool from the down breeds make poor felt. From Norway, comes the Dalasau, and from Holland, the Texel. In Sweden, most of these breeds have been crossed with each other and with the indigenous Swedish breeds, which has caused changes in their characteristics. A cross with a meat breed can be identified generations later by spongy wool. Crossbred wool is called X-wool.

Texel sheep with docked tails.

Wool from Swedish sheep. In each group, there is considerable variation in color, length, thickness, and crimp depending upon the individual and from which part of the sheep the wool was taken.

Top row from left to right: Gute wool and Gotland wool.

Row 2: From the finest Swedish Fin wool to wool of the Gobelin type.

Row 3: White Rya and Spelsau wool in several colors.

Wool from Swedish sheep

Gute Sheep

Gute sheep are Sweden's most ancient sheep breed. In the 1940s, only a few were left on the island of Lilla Karlsö, but today they populate the entire country. Gute wool varies widely in character, from soft to coarse. It is this combination of fiber types within the fleece that makes it excellent for felting, as long as it is shorn twice annually and doesn't self-felt on the sheep. Because it contains abundant kemp hair which spreads out the fibers, making the wool loose, the fleece may appear to have no staple. This type of fleece is ideal for the Mongolian method of preparation by beating the fiber with sticks (see page 24), rather than carding. If the wool is very loose, it can be felted without being beaten. This technique works best for coarse and thick projects such as carpets. The surface of the felt will be smooth whether it is rolled or rubbed on a washboard.

Kemp gives an interesting, slightly rough surface to Gute wool felt, but it is weak and wears apart quickly with use. Kemp hair will break off during the rigors of fulling and will collect at the base of the washboard.

Swedish Fin and Texel wool. Notice the difference in the staple structure, crimp, and luster.

Gute rams have curled horns, another ancient characteristic, and a long mane which can be used uncarded or as a fringe on felt. Even the "eel", the dark wool trim along the middle of the back, can be used uncarded as a design element.

Päls (Gotland) sheep

Päls (Gotland) sheep were bred from Gute sheep in the 1930s and are sometimes called Gotland *utegångsfår* (indicating that they could survive without much human contact). These sheep produce gray pelts with springy and shiny fiber and well-formed distinct locks. Gotland fleeces vary in shade from very light gray to almost black. Through breeding, however, some of the color variation within a fleece has disappeared. Similarly, the outercoat and undercoat have become more homogeneous, especially in length and sheen. If you stretch out a staple, however, you'll see that part of the fiber is shorter and may be of a different color—this is the undercoat. When felting with Gotland wool, it is important to note the appearance of the fleece's undercoat. If it is too similar to the outercoat, the lustrous hair of the outercoat may work its way out of the felt with use, especially if the felt hasn't been fulled hard enough.

Feltmakers have had no impact on the breeding of Gotland sheep to make the wool better for feltmaking. Nevertheless, Gotland wool is easy to felt and is ideal for beginners; the long fibers hold together so well that it can be made into felt within an hour, though it is not very resistant to abrasion. For best results for functional projects, use Gotland fleece that has abundant undercoat fibers. Also choose fleece that is sheared after just six months' growth, which is less likely to be matted and unusable.

Gute ram with handsome mane and "eel" on its back.

Gotland sheep with lambs, whose fleece will become more gray as they age.

Rya sheep.

Rya sheep

Rya sheep are considered to be most similar to the ancient Swedish breed of Viking times. Because of an organized effort to preserve Dalapäls sheep (an indigenous long-wooled sheep found in isolated areas of Dalarna) in the 1920s and a subsequent breeding program, Rya wool is readily available. Today, the efforts of the Rya Club, a society which protects the development and preservation of Rya sheep, are endorsed by the World Nature Foundation.

The outercoat of Rya wool is long and shiny and has large curls or waves. The undercoat, which ideally makes up 40 percent of the weight, is in some cases sufficient in quantity and length to completely bind the outercoat. Rya sheep are most commonly white, but some are black, gray, or brown.

Rya wool has a pleasing sheen. It produces a stiff, strong felt which is ideal for sculpture; protruding pieces can be made to hold their shape without additional stiffening. Uncarded staples can be felted in to form fringe.

If you want a flexible material for felting small sculptures around foam rubber, card a mixture of equal parts Rya and fine wool. The long outercoat and fine undercoat fibers will bind to one another as they are worked on the form.

Rya wool can also be good for hardwearing items such as shoes, boots, seat cushions, and carpets. The lustrous outercoat will give this felt a fine sheen. Lamb's wool can be very soft and is well suited for the outer layers of jackets, where the wool's natural water repellency is put to good use.

Swedish Fin sheep

The Swedish Fin sheep originated from the Finnish Landrace sheep. Lennart Wålstedt, a well-known wool expert who promoted the development of Swedish wools, developed fine wool in Sweden. Known for its fine fiber, the soft wool also has a shiny appearance, which is rare for wool from breeds with fine fiber. The wool has a small, curly crimp. If the wool has fewer than two crimps per centimeter (five crimps per inch), it is classified as Gobelin.

Until recently, Swedish Fin wool has not been used much for felt because it is difficult to handle in the traditional Nordic rubbing method of fulling—the fine fibers tend to shift apart in soapy water. However, the introduction of the rolling technique has allowed this fine wool to be fulled into thin fabric suitable for clothing, cushions, and upholstery. The soft felt is ideal for jewelry and other items that are worn against the skin.

Gobelin-type Swedish Fin wool is good for hats, mittens, jackets, toys, and pictures.

Wool from Swedish Fin sheep may be black or dark brown. Unfortunately, no natural black wool is totally fade resistant. Although coarser wool holds its color longer than fine wool, after a number of years, natural-colored black fleece will bleach out to a brown similar to that of the sun-bleached tips of the clipped fleece.

A drawback of Swedish Fin wool, especially lamb's wool, is that it will nap or pill with repeated handling. To avoid this, see the washing and carding sections (pages 43 and 47).

Swedish Fin sheep are commonly crossed with Texel or English down breeds, which produces sheep with inferior wool for felting. Before you begin to felt, look carefully at the fleece. Swedish Fin fleece typically has a well-defined staple. If the staple in the unwashed fleece looks spongy and undefined, you can assume that the sheep has some meat sheep in its ancestry and that the fleece will be more difficult to work.

Two Swedish Fin lambs. The one on the right has wool of the Gobelin type.

Sheep in the Nordic countries

In addition to the Finnish Landrace, from which Swedish Fin sheep are derived, there are also good "felting sheep" in other parts of the Nordic countries. Like the Swedish Rya sheep, the Landrace sheep in Norway, Iceland, and on the Faeroe Islands have both undercoats and outercoats in their fleece.

In Sweden, the most common of these is the Norwegian Spelsau sheep.

The wool is much like Rya wool but with more kemp. The wool comes in a wide variety of rich color: black, brown, beige, dark gray, gray, and white.

An ancient breed, Villsau, inhabits the islands south of Bergen. Both the rams and ewes are horned and are hardy enough to be left outside year round. The wool is similar to Rya wool but may have a coarser, hairier outercoat and very fine undercoat. The fleece can vary in color from white to dark gray or brown. Villsau wool is difficult to get but delightful to work with.

The Icelandic sheep are similar to the Spelsau, even in terms of color variations, which are many, especially in the red-brown shades.

On the Faeroe Islands today, the sheep are outside year round and are mostly of the Spelsau type. They exhibit the same color range previously mentioned with the exception of black.

Swedish-speaking readers can read more about sheep and wool in the book *Ull*, by Kerstin Gustafsson and Alan Waller.

You don't have to have wool to felt—Angora rabbits, dog hair, mohair, camel, alpaca, etc., can be used for felting. Blend them together with sheep wool or lay a layer of wool underneath the fiber before felting.

Purchasing Wool

Sheep breeders

To locate serious sheep breeders, contact a local sheep club, a district organization of a sheep breeders' association, or your county extension office. Speak with a contact person at these organizations to get tips on which breeders have good wool for handcrafters.

You must be observant when purchasing wool. Some sheep breeders believe that they have purebred sheep, but examination of the wool reveals influence from meat breeds. If you are fortunate enough to locate sheep breeders with a serious interest in wool, you can help them develop even better wool. If a breeder is confident that there will be a market for the wool every year, more attention will be paid to raising purebred sheep, protecting the fleece from vegetable matter, putting sheep in a clean stall the week before they are shorn, shearing them carefully without allowing short cuts of wool to fall in the fleece, and sorting and storing the wool with care.

Commercial carding companies

Establishing a working relationship with a carding company will help you get the quality of wool you want. If you work with large quantities of fleece, provide a sample of the wool type that you want in your batts, for example, fine or medium, to give the processor a reference to work from. The carding company that I employ provides fineness information and a sample staple with their carded batts. This lets me know what type of wool was used.

If a roll of carded batt is labeled only with the breed name, it's more difficult to know the fineness of the wool. Pull some fibers out of the carded batt and lay them on a dark background to determine their length and thickness. With time, you'll be able to identify even carded fiber with your fingers. Save samples of different carded batts along with samples of felt made from them to give you a reference for future orders.

Wool Storage

Wool that is shorn in the autumn is the cleanest. Store wool in paper bags, with newspaper between fleeces, in a dry, airy, cool place. Keep single fleeces in cardboard boxes or paper bags. Don't put the sacks directly on a concrete floor. Avoid plastic bags; they can harbor bacteria and mold which will damage the wool. Mark the packing with all pertinent information so you don't forget where and when the wool was purchased.

Unwashed wool is perishable and must be handled as such. Avoid the temptation to purchase more than you believe can be used within the year. If you cannot use the wool soon, wash it. With time, lanolin and salt on the fiber will degrade, causing the wool staples to break apart. The wool can also become discolored during long periods of storage.

The wool in commercially available carded batts is, as a rule, washed before being carded and therefore has greater tolerance for storage.

Washing Wool and Felt

Traditions and even opinions differ about when wool should be washed, before carding or after felting.

There are many who assert that the sheep's lanolin and sweat help the felting process, and indeed, it is true that if water used is warm enough to loosen the lanolin, the soap formed from the sheep's own products contributes to the fiber's migration during felting. On the other hand, saponified oil soap (see page 58) performs the same function. Large quantities of dirt in the wool may prevent the fibers from felting to one another.

There are others who believe strongly that wool should be washed before being felted. Residual dirt can make wool difficult to card and felt. You want to avoid getting dirt in your hand carders or carding machine (it can clog the teeth), lungs (it can cause respiratory problems), or in the cloth and bamboo mats (it can cause them to deteriorate).

Swedish Fin wool should be washed before it is carded even if it appears clean. Small balls of fiber can easily form in the batt, preventing a smooth layer of carded wool from being formed. My theory is that lanolin causes the finest and shortest fibers to cling to one another and form little balls. No matter what the reason, you'll have much better results if the wool has been washed. The fibers of this wool can also be somewhat weak, especially at the thinner tips of lamb's wool, which have been exposed to sun and abrasion. If these weak fibers are clumped together with lanolin and dirt, they will break off during carding.

As lanolin ages, it will make the wool difficult to card and may cause discoloration. Always wash wool that you plan to store for more than one year. This is especially important if the wool will not be stored under cool, dry conditions.

Because moth larvae prefer dirty wool, clean wool is less susceptible to moth damage.

Another risk of dirty wool is the appearance of dirt stains in large felt items which are rolled for several days. When the roll lies in one place overnight, gravity will cause the dirt particles to move down to the bottom of the roll. In some cases they will leave dark lines or streaks which are very difficult to remove.

Washing can be done in different ways with different degrees of effectiveness, from a thorough scouring to remove all of the lanolin to a light rinsing. Here are some suggestions:

Cold water without a washing agent

This will leave the lanolin in the wool but remove much of the dirt. Use this method for lightly soiled wool before carding and for wool that will be stored for some time.

Let the wool soak in cool water (about 35°C/95°F) for 10 minutes. Rinse the wool in fresh water of the same temperature until the water remains clear.

Warm Water without a Washing Agent

This will remove about 80 percent of the lanolin and dirt. Use this method for very dirty wool before carding and for wool that will be stored for a long period of time.

Let the wool soak in hot water (about 45°C/113°F) for 10 minutes to allow the calcium salts and the fatty acids in the wool to make a soap. This soap will loosen more of the lanolin in the wool. The water must be kept at at least 40°C (104°F) for the soak to be effective. Rinse the wool in fresh water of the same temperature until the water remains clear.

Warm water with a washing agent

This will scour the wool completely. Use this method for wool and felt that will be dyed and for felt cloth that is completely fulled.

Most craft stores that sell wool dyes also sell an assortment of special wool-washing agents. Environmentally friendly dish detergents (with a neutral pH of about 7) or shampoo can also be used.

Wool that is to be dyed must be washed well because the dye will attach only to clean fibers. If you accept (or even desire) a little color variation between the root and tip of the staple, you can follow the method described above for washing in warm water without a washing agent. Most of the remaining lanolin will dissolve in the hot dyebath, but the color will not be even.

Dissolve a washing agent in warm water (40°C/104°F), add the wool, and let it soak for 10 minutes. Rinse the wool at least three times with water of the same temperature, or until the water remains clear.

Put a dash of vinegar in the last rinse to neutralize any remaining alkalinity.

All finished felt items need a light wash to remove the felting solution, even if washed wool was used. This is especially true if saponified oil soap was used. If not thoroughly rinsed out, this soap residue will cause felt to turn yellow with time. Saponified oil soap is very alkaline, with a pH of 10.2 in a normal (1%) solution, which can cause the fiber to gradually deteriorate. For the final wash, use lukewarm water (about 37°C/99°F) and a small amount of fine washing agent or neutral dish detergent with a pH of about 7. Move the object up and down in a large basin of water. Don't squeeze the felt to remove the excess water, but spin it in a washing machine for half a minute. (*Translator's note: To restore the wool felt to its normal acidic pH, soak it in a rinse bath to which a dash of vinegar has been added for 15 minutes before a final rinse in clear water.*)

General Instructions for All Types of Wool Washing

1. Fill a washtub, bucket, or sink with water. Don't let the water run directly onto the wool: the running water could cause felting. Add the washing agent.

2. Add the wool and press it carefully down into the water. Add small amounts of wool at a time. If your wool separates easily into staples, place it in a net bag before submerging it in the water.

3. Let the wool soak in the water for about 10 minutes. Don't squeeze the wool: this can cause felting. Carefully lift the wool up a few times to allow the water to circulate through the fleece. To prevent the lanolin from depositing on the wool, remove the wool before the water temperature cools. Drain off the water and lift the wool out of the basin.

4. Fill the basin with clean rinse water of the same temperature as the wash water. (Don't shock the wool by drastically changing the water temperature.) Gently place the wool in the water. Continue rinsing in fresh water until the water remains clear.

5. Spin out the wool in a washing machine for several seconds to remove excess soap, dirt, and water. Do not use a dryer, which can cause the wool to felt.

6. Dry the clean wool on newspaper, net, or a drying rack. Shake the wool pieces and separate them to allow maximum air circulation. Mesh trays that sit above one another in a frame are excellent for drying a lot of wool in a small space. I have found that wool dries fastest if I lay newspaper on the bottom of the trays and replace the newspaper every now and then. Otherwise, water collects in the bottom and keeps the wool wet. During warm weather, dry the wool outside out of direct sunlight, which can make the fiber brittle.

Dyeing

When I began felting, I was fascinated by the natural colors of wool, but with time, I became interested in using dyes to create special color nuances. Fleece, carded batts, and felt can be dyed with plants and mushrooms as long as the vegetable material has been strained out of the dyebath. Plant dyes are sufficiently lightfast, although yellow tones will fade if exposed to constant light. Synthetic dyes will usually not fade.

The various types of dyes are distinguished by their method of handling. Cotton dyes, also called batik dyes, are not suited for wool; they are strongly alkaline and will corrode the wool. I don't recommend "all-purpose dyes" because they are not very wash- or lightfast.

The best dyes are those designed for wool: wool dyes, acid dyes, and metal-complex dyes. Because the industrial product name is seldom used in the retail trade, a range of colors from one retailer can contain many different types of dyes. For example, a yellow might be an acid dye while the red might be metal-complex. If you desire a high degree of fastness to light, washing, and abrasion, choose a dye made specifically for wool.

Wool dyes can also be used for printing and painting on wool (as well as on silk). There's an advantage to having a single dye that can be used for different application methods. In their unmixed form, these dyes have a shelf life of several years.

Workplace

Small amounts of fleece or fabric can be dyed on the stove in your kitchen. Remember that dyestuffs are toxic and that all food should be put away before you begin. Also be sure to clean up any spills immediately.

Work in a well-ventilated area near a water source and drain. With a hot plate on a table and with plastic on the floor underneath, you can dye nearly anywhere you want.

Dyeing Felt Objects, Small and Large

For a project in a single color, dye the finished cloth or piece rather than the fleece or carded batts. A project that has a pattern in black on a light-colored background can also be dyed afterward. The areas of black will absorb a bit of the dyebath, which can be an advantage.

Even multicolored garments with soft gradations between colors can be dyed after felting. Hang the cloth or object on two stakes which are suspended over the kettle, so that just a part of the felt is in the bath. This area will take the dye. After the dyeing is complete, shift the fabric and suspend it over a new dyebath so that another color will overlap the first. You can gradually shift from one color to another in this way.

A very large sculpture can also be dyed in stages in a similar way by dipping it in the dyebath. Be very careful that the boundaries between the areas being dyed don't get a double dose of dye. Continuously move the project up and down a little as you dip it so that a sharp line doesn't form where it meets the surface of the water.

Variations

Try the following variations for stunning effects.

1. Use an assortment of shades of gray wool. The dye will produce an assortment of lovely soft tones.

2. Mix two or three colors of dye in the dyebath.

3. Make subtle color nuances by removing the wool, adding a different color to the dyebath, a little bit at a time, and adding new wool with each new color.

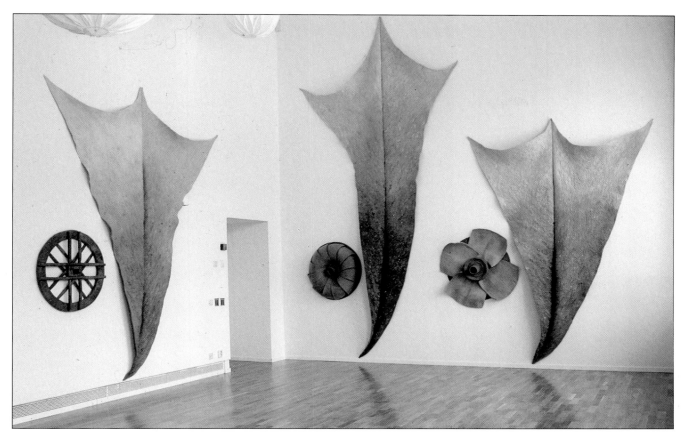

Power, by Gunilla Paetau Sjöberg. The largest form is 2.5 × 5 m (8¹/₄ × 16¹/₂ ft). After being felted, the tall forms were dyed in sections following the simple dyeing method with acid/metal-complex dyes. The dye progression was judged visually as the dyeing progressed. Dyed wool staple was laid onto undyed fleece before felting to create interesting surface variation. These were then overdyed. Rya wool gives the shapes stability.

The work is in the conference room of the Älvkarleby power/heating plant.

4. Rainbow-dye the wool by putting several dye colors into the bath, but not mixing them, so that the wool will take up the different colors in different areas.

5. Overdye one color on top of another. For example, dye the fiber in a blue bath and then in a red bath to get exactly the shade of blue-red you want.

6. Use string, rubber bands, etc., to knot around the felt, especially thin felt, to create a resist pattern as in tie-dyeing. Read more about this technique in books about tie-dyeing.

7. Card together batches of wool dyed different colors.

8. Felt together thin layers of different colors.

Printing and Painting

There are many dyes for printing and painting that also work on felt. For best results in printing on felt, the surface should have a dense, smooth texture, such as is produced by a fine wool. Ideally, the felt should be made with the rolling technique, which produces the tightest and smoothest surface possible. If the felt was fulled in the washing machine, it should be passed through a mangle or steam pressed by a reputable dry cleaner. The lumpier and hairier the felt, the more difficult it will be to obtain sharp edges on the pattern shapes.

Simple stencil printing

Stenciling is simple and effective. Make a stencil out of firm plastic and fasten it securely to the felt with freezer tape along at least two sides. Pour a little thickened dye into a dish and cover this with a piece of thin foam rubber. This will be your printing pad. Roll up yet another piece of foam rubber to make a stencil sponge or dauber. Secure the roll with a rubber band. You can also use a paintbrush for stencil printing, but it will be more difficult to get an even print.

Press the dauber down into the dye on the printing pad. Then press the dye-filled dauber firmly into the opening in the stencil so that the dye squishes down into the fiber. Repeat until the dye completely covers the fiber in the stencil opening. Fix the dye according to the manufacturer's directions.

Painting

You can paint felt by using a small, stiff paintbrush to press the dye down into the fiber, but it is not easy to create fine, even lines on a hairy surface. Practice before painting a large project. You may find it easier to make a stencil of small lines instead of painting freehand. With a dauber, you can also "paint" the surface with different dots.

Khyber Pass. **Patricia Spark,** Albany, Oregon. Pat has experimented with color by dyeing fleece and then carding it into color progressions for feltmaking. When she wants to have pure colors on top of one another in a felt wall hanging, she first makes several pieces of felt in which the fleece is carded from one color to another. Afterward, the pieces are cut out of the felt and appliquéd over one another so that during felting the colors of one layer do not affect the colors of the others. In this piece, a layer of gray wool was put under the brighter-colored wool in the background to tone down the bright colors.

Khyber Pass is about the flight of nomadic people from Afghanistan to Pakistan during the Soviet invasions. The intense colors represent the feelings of fright and despair.

Inge Evers, Haarlem, Holland, is an artist and instructor. Her shaman's cloak was rainbow-dyed with fiber-reactive dyes, though it could also be done with acid and metal-complex dyes. The cloak is made from three long pieces of felt made of silk and wool felted together. The fabric was about 4 meters (13 feet) long, and was draped and sewed together. Magical objects were sewed to the outside strip of felt.

The detail picture of Inge's shaman's cloak shows her different techniques.

• Silk, which is dyed in a single multicolored dyebath, is draped over the shaman's "head".

• The same multicolored silk was felted onto the wool used in the middle section of the cloak. Silk was also used to create a pattern on the surface of the felt.

• The red section is made of silk chiffon that was dyed red, pink, and orange, and then felted onto a red-violet wool.

• The dark blue section is made of three layers: half-moon shapes of silk fiber, dark gray silk gauze, and red, brown, orange, and purple wool. These layers were felted together with the rolling technique in a bamboo mat.

Carding

To make a thin and even felt, you must have well-carded wool, but there are cases in which a simpler method of processing wool is sufficient.

Prepare the Wool

Begin by washing the wool (see page 43). For best results, the wool should be warm when it is carded so that the lanolin is soft. Warm wool by placing it in a basket near a radiator, in front of an open oven, or on a newspaper on the open oven door. You may find it pleasant to warm the wool, as well as yourself, in the sun as you card the wool outdoors.

Blending wool types

Blending wool types is as important in felting as it is for spinning and weaving. Wool from different parts of the sheep (or even from different sheep) must be blended to minimize the risk of differential shrinkage. For small projects, however, you can use just the part of the fleece that would be best for the result desired.

For large projects, such as fabric for a jacket, select wool that has similar characteristics from several fleeces and blend them, or thoroughly blend all of the different fleece types from a single sheep. Sorting the wool according to quality and using a pinch of each type for each batch to be carded will thoroughly blend the various types of wool. In the past, wool was always carded twice at the carding bench. For the second carding, the felter held a number of carded batts from the first carding under his or her arm and pulled out tufts of fiber from them as needed. Instead of pulling tufts, you can lay the carded batts in a stack on the kitchen floor and beat them with a stick to break them apart and blend them.

Traditionally, white and black wool were carded together to make gray. The two colors should be blended together well enough that neither is dominant in the mixture.

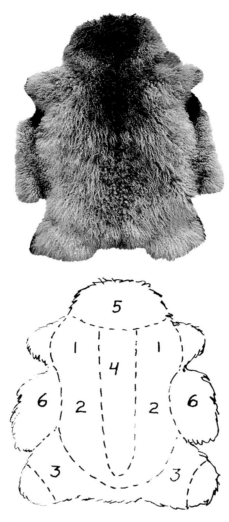

The character of the wool varies throughout a pelt. The best wool comes from the shoulders (1) and the sides (2). Wool from the haunches (3) is considerably coarser. The back wool (4) is more open and loose. The neck wool (5) can be soft and more finely fibered than the rest of the fleece. The belly wool (6) is more open, tangled, and often full of vegetable matter. The leg wool is short and coarse.

For thicker projects such as carpets, simplify the process of blending various qualities of wool by using a different type of wool in each layer. This will create layers that each have different characteris-

tics, for example a jacket fabric that has a long-fibered, water-resistant surface and a soft "lining".

When Carding is Not Necessary

Carding is not always necessary if you use a properly loosened Gute fleece that lacks a distinct staple. In this case, you don't need to beat the wool with a stick; you can use the wool right from the pelt. If you want to felt a large project such as a cushion or rug, straighten the wool staples by pulling them directly out of the fleece, and lay them out as the Mongolians do (see pages 25–26). Even with this crude approach, it is a good idea to use fiber that has been sorted according to its characteristics.

Teasing

Teasing is a simple method of separating wool staples with the fingers that is especially appropriate for children. Because the method takes a long time, it is best for small projects. Hold the staple lengthwise in one hand and pull it to the side with the other hand to separate it into a fluffy cloud. Use the Mongolian method of laying out the teased wool for felting (see pages 25–26).

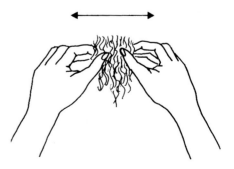

Teasing wool.

Stick Beating

Staples can be fluffed by beating them with a stick. Gute wool is the best Swedish wool for this kind of processing, but other coarse wools such as Karakul can also be used. Fleece that has a well-defined staple but that is slightly matted benefits from stick beating. Beating loosens the staple and forces out some dirt. And it's fun! Lay the wool in a pile on a tarp or rush mat and with a slender willow stick (approximately 1 meter (1 yard) long) in each hand, beat the wool rhythmically to fluff it. Then lay out the wool in the Mongolian method.

Carding Bow

The carding bow is an ancient tool that was originally used to fluff cotton. It is thought to have originated in China but is used in many other Asiatic countries as well, with the exception of Mongolia, for fluffing wool. It has been in popular use as far west as Finland and has been used by hatmakers through time.

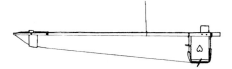

The carding bow looks like a 2-m (6¹⁄₂-ft)-long double-bass bow. A simpler variety looks like an archer's bow. The strings are made from twisted animal gut and are put into vibration with a mallet or a bowing pin.

Hand Carders

Carding with hand carders is a peaceful activity, though it takes time. It is ideal for small felt projects that need to be thin and uniform, such as mittens.

To begin to use hand carders, sit comfortably with good back support. Lay the bottom carder on your left knee with the handle pointing away from you and the teeth facing up. Hold the handle with your left hand. Hold the top carder with your right hand with the teeth facing down. Keep your right leg out of the way of the top carder. Eventually, you can lay your left leg over your right if it feels comfortable.

The finished wool batts can be laid in a box or between sheets of newspaper. Place a washboard on top of the layers to press the air out of the wool.

Beat wool with willow branches that are 1.5 to 2 centimeters (1/2 to 3/4 inch) in diameter. (Bamboo rods from woven window blinds can also be used.) Choose an area sheltered from wind and beat with both sticks at once or alternate between the two.

1. Charge the bottom carder

Charge the bottom carder by placing small clumps of fleece near the handle and pulling them along the teeth in the carding cloth. Press them in gently so that they are caught by the teeth. Don't overload the carder.

2. The first carding pass

With the carders parallel to one another, set the upper carder's top edge in the middle of the bottom carder and pull it against the wool. Pass the carders across each other, pressing them together just enough to pull the wool between them; do not press so hard that the teeth engage. With each pass, some of the wool from the bottom carder will be transferred to the upper carder. Proper alignment of the carders is essential. If the carders are passed at an angle to each other, the wool will be incorrectly lodged and the upper edge of the top carder will be ruined; if the top carder is held obliquely, the teeth will be ruined.

On the next pass, start with the upper carder a little closer to the handle of the bottom carder. Card with soft, rhythmic, circular steps. Don't make more than four or five passes before you turn the wool over (see below). It is more effective to turn the wool often than to make many passes with the carders.

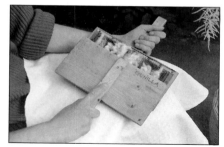

3. Clear the lower carder—left carder

After a few passes, some of the wool will have been transferred from the bottom (left) carder to the upper (right) carder.

Turn the right carder so that the teeth face up. Rotate the lower carder toward you so that the teeth face down and the handle is toward you. Place the left carder at an angle against the right carder's inner (handle) edge and shove it forward to make the wool remaining on the left carder shift to the right carder.

Turn the left carder around and place it back on your knee. Also turn the right carder so that the teeth face down again. You can do this without letting go of the carders; they will still be in the same hands you began with.

Card three or four times. Remove any chaff and second cuts (small bits of fleece that have been cut off the staple during shearing) that appear.

4. Clear the upper carder—right carder

The wool should now be turned so that it shifts over from the upper carder to the lower carder, that is, from the right to the left carder.

Turn the carders as you did to shift the wool from the bottom carder to the upper carder. But this time, angle the outer edge (the edge away from the handle) of the right carder against the inner edge (handle edge) of the left carder. Push the right carder from the inner edge to the outer edge of the left carder. All of the wool will be transferred to the left carder, which is laid back down on your knee for further carding. Continue to card and turn the wool by clearing it from the upper and lower carders alternately until the wool forms a fine, even batt.

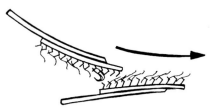

Left carder. Clearing the left carder.

Right carder. Clearing the right carder.

5. Remove the carded batt

When the wool has been thoroughly carded, clear the upper carder as described above so that the wool is on the bottom carder. Then pull the upper carder back against the lower carder as if you were going to clear the lower carder, but very lightly, without pressure. The wool batt will be lightly fastened to the upper carder. Pull the upper carder containing the wool batt very lightly back over the bottom carder once more. This should loosen the wool batt from the teeth so that you can easily lift it off. Lift off the batt in the direction of the carding teeth so that it will not get caught by them.

The Carding Bench

A carding bench, also called a carding chair, is a very effective tool for carding. In the old days, this preparation was called "scrubbing the wool". It produces well-carded wool and is considerably quicker than hand carders. The face of the lower carder is larger than a hand carder and is tightly fastened to the bench. The upper carder is held with both hands and can be used with more force than a hand carder. The carding bench was used extensively in Sweden for carding wool in preparation for felting.

If you purchase a carding bench, choose a model with a slightly curved carding face. A curved face is easier to work with than a flat one.

1. Charge the lower carding face

Lay the wool on the lower carder face as with hand carders. If the wool is short and the carding face is large, you can put two rows of fleece on the face. Card the same way as described for hand carding, but turn the wool as described below. Card about five times.

2. Clear the upper carder

Turn the upper carder so that the handle points away from you. Set the upper carder's handleless edge on the far edge of the lower card, angle it up a little, and pull the carder toward you so that the wool adheres to the lower carder face.

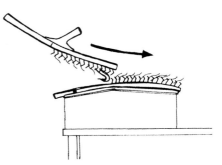

Clearing the upper carder.

3. Clear the lower carder

Turn the upper carder so that the handle points away from you again. Set the upper carder's handled edge on the near edge of the lower carder, and push the upper carder away from you so that the wool is transferred onto the upper carder.

Continue to card and turn the wool, repeating steps 1, 2, and 3.

4. Remove the carded batt

In one swipe, make the two types of clearing/turning motions so that the batt loosens and lies on top of the lower carder. Remove it with both hands, keeping the length of the fiber parallel to the teeth as you pull it off.

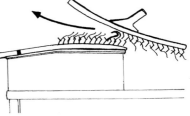

Clearing the lower carder.

Drum Carders

There are many types of drum carders, both manual and electrical, all of which speed the carding process. If you plan to make felt for clothing fabric, however, you may be better off purchasing carded batts from a carding company as it is difficult to produce large quantities of fine, even batts from fine wool on a hand-driven drum carder. When using a drum carder, weigh out the fleece in equal-sized bits before carding so that the batts will be the same thickness.

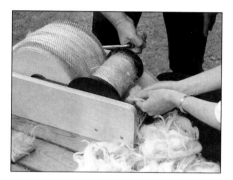

For best results (and more fun!), a hand-driven drum carder can be worked by two people, one who feeds in the wool and the other who turns the crank. Feed in just a little wool at a time and hold it back gently so that the drum doesn't get clogged. When the large drum is full, use a rod to make a separation in the batt and then roll the batt off. Most crimpy wool will need to pass through the drum carder twice. The small drum should only be cleared if another color of fleece is to be used.

Moths and Carpet Beetles

Moths and carpet beetles appreciate fine wool as much as we do. The wool worker must find ways to keep them out of both working materials and finished products.

Moths are the greatest menace because under favorable conditions they can multiply quickly and the larvae can wreak substantial damage in a very short time. Read about moths on page 52. Carpet beetles can also be unpleasant, but they usually appear as individuals, unless they breed in a dead mouse or other animal nearby.

Mothproofing the Wool

Through proper care of the fiber and wool products, you can hold damaging insects at bay without using chemicals. Moths seldom establish themselves in clothing that is worn regularly. It is a more difficult situation for textile artists who cannot protect large works, especially ones that hang in public locations beyond their control. Here, carpet beetles are the largest problem. Mothproofing agents also deter carpet beetles if the dose is at least doubled.

Preventive Measures

Moths and carpet beetles commonly find their way into the workplace and storeroom through infested wool. Because carpet beetles fly through the air in the spring, be sure to store wool in rooms that have screens on the windows. Some moths live in birds' nests and can fly into the house, but these moths don't pose a great threat.

Take charge of the wool
- Keep an eye out for moths in newly purchased wool.

- Only buy as much wool as you can use in a year.
- Store wool under cool temperatures to hinder moth reproduction.
- Seal all wool storage bags to prevent the spread of moths.
- Wash wool that will be stored for a long time. Newly hatched moth larvae feed on lanolin as well as keratin (wool protein) and will migrate to the dirty parts of fleece and wool.
- Spray the opening of the wool storage sack and the top layer of wool with an insecticide containing pyrethrum or allethrin if there is evidence of moths. The active ingredient is effective for up to six months.
- Check wool storage bags frequently for evidence of moths, especially in the spring when moths are most active.
- Watch for flying moths. Although females do not fly well, a single flying male moth is an indication of egg-laying females and hungry larvae nearby.

Protecting felted projects
- There are many reasons to air items made of wool, not the least of which is that moth eggs are damaged by sunlight and cold. A sunny winter day with a temperature of –20°C (–4°F) is excellent for airing wool garments, carpets, and wall hangings.
- Clean closets regularly and spray the corners and molding with an insect repellent if moths have been present.
- Wear wool garments regularly to discourage moth activity.
- Wash soiled wool garments and other items promptly.

Combating infestation
- If you find a moth, examine all wool storage bags and wool items. Be sure to check the bottom of the bags and behind seams.
- If the infestation is restricted to a small amount of wool, immerse it in water at at least 60°C (140°F) for a minimum of 10 minutes to kill all stages of the insect. Or wash and dye the wool at a temperature greater than 60°C (140°F).

Alternatively, freeze the infested wool to a temperature of at least –18°C (0°F) for a minimum of two days. Large amounts of wool may take as long as a week to freeze to this temperature. To speed the process, divide large quantities of wool into several smaller bags. These extreme temperatures are necessary to thoroughly destroy all stages of moths.

- A very hot sauna, set at 80°C (176°F), is excellent for killing moths. An oven can be used for smaller pieces. Spread out the fabric so that the heat is distributed evenly. Even moth eggs will die at temperatures above 56°C (133°F).
- Moth eggs, which are very fragile, can be destroyed by vigorous brushing. However, the surface of most felt is too hairy to be brushed successfully.
- If the fabric is severely infested, wrap it up in plastic and throw it away.
- Clean the moth-infested area thoroughly. Vacuum, scour, and spray the area, including shelves and drawers, with insecticide. Moth larvae can fasten their pupae on walls and in cracks in the floor. Spray three times at two-week intervals.
- If the moths return despite these precautions, hire a professional exterminator.

Facts about clothes moths

Moth. Length: 5 to 8 mm (1/6 to 3/8 inch). Wingspan: 10 to 17 mm (1/2 to 3/4 inch). Color: golden yellow to grayish yellow. Light shy, the females hop and jump rather than fly. Eggs are laid in dark areas of fleece, woolens, and furs, one to eight days after the moth breaks out of the cocoon. The female dies after all of her eggs have been laid, which can take up to seventeen days, depending on the temperature. The male lives ten to forty-five days.

Egg. Size: barely visible at 0.3 by 0.5 mm (1/100 to 1/60 in). Color: white. The eggs lie loose and are not fastened to the wool. A female can lay 25 to 100 eggs, which at 75% humidity will hatch after twenty-four days at 15°C (59°F), after ten days at 20°C (68°F), after seven days at 25°C (77°F), and after six days at 30°C (86°F). The eggs die at temperatures above 50°C (122°F).

Larva. Size: newly hatched: 0.2 mm (1/150 in) wide by 1 mm (1/16 inch) long; fully grown: up to 12 mm (1/2 inch) long. Color: white with brown head. Larvae borings and excrement are left in the wool. The borings are about ten times longer than the larvae. The larva can shed its skin up to forty-five times. It can go into a dormant stage if temperature and diet deterio-

rate. They can live up to four years. Pupation occurs at 15°C (59°F) after 186 to 195 days, at 20°C (68°F) after 123 to 135 days, and at 25°C (77°F) after 72 to 89 days, at 70% relative humidity.

The larva require nutrient-rich additives, such as lanolin, in addition to keratin (in hair and feathers). Older larvae can live partially on hair or wool. Better food sources will produce pupation more quickly. At 25°C (77°F), pupation can occur in just 45 to 50 days. If the temperature is lower than 10°C (50°F) or above 35°C (95°F), the moth cannot complete its life cycle.

With repeated temperature fluctuations between 0°C (32°F) and –5°C (23°F) or a few times freezing below –10°C (14°F), all moth stages will die.

Pupa. Length: 4 to 7 mm (1/6 to 1/4 inch). The limp, yellowish cocoon is spun with remains of wool and excrement. At 70 percent humidity, the moth will emerge after 35 days at 15°C (59°F), 18 days at 20°C (68°F), 12 days at 25°C (77°F), and 10 days at 30°C (86°F).

Generations. The number of generations vary, from four to five per year to a single generation every four years, depending on the climate and food source.

Clothes moth.

Clothes moth larvae and their excrement.

Carpet beetle larva and pupa.

Allergies and Other Problems

The occurrences of allergies and asthma have increased considerably over the past few years, and there are those who believe that wool is partly to blame. To research this problem, I interviewed Dr. Tony Foucard, a specialist in child and youth allergies, and Dr. Magnus Lindberg, a specialist in work-related skin diseases. Both doctors work at the Academy Hospital in Uppsala, Sweden.

Clean Wool Poses No Danger

A clean wool fiber will not evoke an allergic reaction or asthma attack. On the other hand, wool that was not washed soon after shearing can trap skin particles and other allergens that can make a sensitized person very sick.

Therefore, always work with unwashed wool in restricted locations, for example, in the textile studio of a school, not a regular classroom. While the unwashed wool is being handled, children with allergies can be taken to another area. The textile studio should be cleaned before being used by another group which might include allergic children. This is very important because even a little allergen can evoke a serious reaction. Alternatively, use scrupulously clean wool.

Dust on Felt Items

All hairy surfaces, including wool, gather dust, although possibly to a lesser extent than synthetic fibers, which attract dust with their static electricity. Dust is responsible for many allergies, and therefore all publicly displayed felt items should be periodically vacuumed or dusted.

Eczema on the Hands

It is not uncommon for a feltmaker's hands to be afflicted with dermatitis. Water, felting solutions, and washing agents remove the protective oils from the skin, allowing it to be irritated by bacteria, dirt, and chemicals, and resulting in what some people call "wear and tear" eczema.

To protect your hands, apply hand cream after every contact with water or, better yet, wear rubber gloves.

Wool Clothing

Some people are very sensitive to wool against the skin, especially the coarser and stiffer fibers that stick out and irritate the skin. Lamb's wool from the finest Swedish Fin sheep, in which only one end of the fiber is cut, is much less irritating than other wools. Protect sensitive skin by wearing a cotton garment beneath the wool.

Wool has largely the same composition as human skin. Wool clothing is breathable, warm, and it insulates against dampness. There is no reason why very small children should not wear wool garments, unless of course, they suffer from dermatitis.

Because it is difficult to disinfect wool cloth and retain the wool's primary characteristics, delicate washing by hand is recommended for garments used at home.

Felting Techniques

When Wool Becomes Felt

Hatmakers boast that their patron saint, Saint Clement, the fourth bishop of Rome, invented the art of feltmaking when he placed wool in his sandals to cushion his feet as he traveled. When he removed his sandals, the wool had turned to felt. But felting was already well established as handwork when Saint Clement lived. Another tale is that the savage horsemen of Asia invented felt saddle blankets by laying wool under their saddles to protect their horses' backs from abrasion by the saddle. These stories are made credible by their inclusion of all the necessary ingredients to make felt: wool, moisture, warmth, and agitation.

Characteristics of wool fiber

Wool has the unique ability to felt to itself. During felting, wool fibers migrate and entangle with one another. The epidermal scales covering the fibers overlap like shingles, allowing the fibers to easily glide forward past one another without sliding back. With agitation, the fibers entangle as one fiber bends around another and becomes locked in place by the scales. With continued agitation, the fibers catch and cling to one another, and felting begins.

Carding prepares the fibers for felting by forcing the fibers to bend a little as they arch around the carder teeth. Because fibers that have been combed are in a more parallel alignment, they do not entangle with each other as easily and therefore do not felt as readily.

When laying out carded wool for felting, you can increase the likelihood of entanglement by using at least two layers

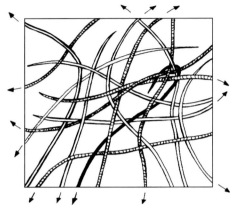

Felt is made up of fibers. Felting begins when one fiber twists around its neighbors and is held in place by its scales. As the fiber rotates through agitation, it pulls the others together, causing them to lock onto each other in a similar fashion.

of wool with the fibers oriented perpendicular to each other.

The structure and texture of the wool fiber are the key to its ability to form felt. Fibers with well-formed scales will migrate forward easily and will not slip backwards. Thin, soft fibers will bend more easily around each other than will coarse, stiff (outercoat) fibers. Because fine wool has more fine fibers per square centimeter (one-quarter square inch) to entangle with each other, it will felt more readily. To produce a durable and tight felt with coarse wool fibers, blend them with fine fibers. Coarse fiber can, on the other hand, function as armor to strengthen batts of short fiber. In the early stages of feltmaking, coarse fibers can prevent the short fibers from slipping apart.

Another important characteristic for felting is the elasticity of the fiber, that is, its ability to resume its shape after being

stretched. Elasticity contributes to the fiber's ability to migrate in the wool batts. Wool from some meat breeds (Texel, for example) are so elastic that it is difficult to felt. The spiral crimp in the fibers makes them tend to spring out in all directions instead of clinging to one another.

If you want to mix wool with another fiber that does not felt, such as cotton, use a fine wool fiber for best results. Of course, the more wool you use, the more durable the felt will be. Some fibers, such as flax, will felt more easily when mixed with wool.

Moisture

Moisture is an essential component for felting. When wool fiber is wet, the microscopic canals in the cortex layer fill with water. The canals swell and shorten, causing the scales to push outward, even in the presence of a small amount of water. Because excessive amounts of water can prevent the fibers from coming in contact with one another, excess water should be allowed to drain away from the fibers as they are felted.

Soap or acid—pH conditions for the felting solution

As a beginning felter, I read with great astonishment that hatmakers added sulfuric acid to their felting solutions. They never used soap, which acts both as an adhesive to hold the fibers together in the beginning of the process and as a lubricant to promote migration of the fibers. It turns out that acid behaves just like soap to promote swelling of the wool fibers in water. Either acidic or alkaline solutions will cause wool fibers to swell and scales to open, thereby encouraging the felting process.

At pH 4.9, wool is the most stable and tolerant of chemicals. The fibers are least apt to swell and felt at pH levels between 3 and 6.

The best pH conditions for felting occur in acidic solutions with pH levels between 1 and 2 and in basic solutions with pH levels between 10 and 11. A liter (4¼ cups) of water mixed with 10 milliliters (2 teaspoons) of saponified oil soap has a pH of 10.2. At pH levels above 12, the fibers will swell without limits and break down if they are heated.

The amount of soap to be added depends on the softness of the water and whether or not the wool has been washed. Clean wool requires more soap because the natural lanolin and salts have been removed. Take care not to use too much soap, though; too much lather can prevent the fibers from coming in contact with one another. It is possible to felt wool without soap or other additives—it just takes longer!

Temperature

Water temperature will determine how quickly the wool will felt. In an alkaline solution, the ideal felting temperature is between 40° and 50°C (104° and 122°F). In practical terms, you should use water as hot as possible. The wool will begin to swell as soon as the water is poured over it. Alkaline felting solutions at temperatures above 45°C (113°F) will defeat the wool's elastic tendencies, preventing the fibers from returning to their original size after being extended.

In an acidic solution, felting is promoted by increased heat. Therefore hat-makers often work next to a stove where the felting solution is kept hot.

Some feltmakers shock the fiber by alternating between warm and cold water. This technique produces a fabric that is suitable for carpets but is not recommended for garments. Shocking the wool causes the scales to spread out in the fibers, making them harsh.

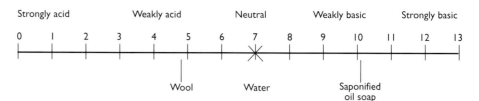

pH scale from acidic to alkaline, with 7 being neutral. At pH levels of about 4.9, wool is most resistant to chemicals. Saponified oil soap mixed with water in ordinary concentrations has a pH of 10.2. Wool fiber swells the most between pH 1 and 2 and between pH 10 and 11, which are also the best conditions for felting.

Agitation

Agitation, i.e., pressure and movement, is required for felting to occur. Pressure forces the air out of the fleece so that the fibers can come in contact with one another. Movement, which in the beginning consists of careful massage and circular motions, allows the fibers to migrate to produce a thin, stretchable felt. This phase is called felting. During the fulling phase, the fibers are further compacted by hard rubbing and rolling to produce rigid felt. It is during the fulling phase that shrinking and shaping take place. To get an extremely hard felt, use a wooden felting board and mallet to compact the fibers and minimize the spaces between them. During this phase, it is possible for the fibers in some types of wool to regain their wavy structure as they are worked against one another, forming a bumpy or buckling surface (called a pebble surface).

When using the Swedish rubbing technique (see page 61), take care to form a single cohesive unit. If you begin fulling too quickly, the felt will be uneven and unnecessarily thick. When using the rolling technique (see page 64), felting and fulling are done simultaneously. You will need to stretch the felt to make it thin or to get the desired shape, for example, the brim of a hat. And don't be in a hurry! There is no shortcut to good felt!

Shrinkage

All of the descriptions of felted objects in this book include only approximations of the amount of fiber used and its shrinkage. This is because felting is not an exact technique. There are no strict rules. Perhaps the charm of felting is that each project is a function of the type of fleece used, the thickness of the layers, and the degree of fulling.

In terms of shrinkage, we can say that
- Finely fibered wool shrinks more than coarse fibers.
- Batts that are laid out in thin layers will shrink more than batts laid out in thick layers.
- The rolling technique causes less shrinkage than the rubbing technique.
- Felt shrinks most when it is fulled in a washing machine.

We can say in general that Rya wool shrinks 35 percent and Swedish Fin wool shrinks 45 percent, but there are qualifications. The amount of shrinkage depends on how fine the fibers are, how much undercoat is in a fleece, the thickness of the carded batts, which felting technique is used, and the density of the felt.

After you have a feel for these variables, you can experiment with a single wool type to compare how they affect shrinkage. For example, compare batts of different thickness and different felting techniques.

Through the process of felting, you have the opportunity to learn how to feel and look for wool qualities. All of the hard work has its rewards!

You may come to the following conclusions:

- Wool laid out in thin layers will produce a thinner and tighter felt than will wool laid out in thick layers.
- Several thin layers stacked in a crisscross fashion will produce a tighter felt than will two thick layers.
- Fine-fibered wool will make a thinner felt than will coarse-fibered wool.
- When the rolling technique is used, the felt on the inside of the roll will shrink more than the felt on the outside of the roll.

Figuring shrinkage

The exact percentage of shrinkage must be figured if you want your project to have a predetermined size. To do this, make a sample with the wool that you plan to use in your project. Lay out the wool on a marked, square surface, for example 30 centimeters (12 inches) square, to the thickness you think you will need. Press down on the wool so that the layers hold together, roll them into a bundle, and weigh the bundle. For our example, let's assume it weighs 28 grams (1 ounce). (You will need to know this to calculate the amount of wool you'll need.) Lay any decorations on the wool and felt with the technique that you plan to use.

To figure the shrinkage, divide the dimension of the laid-out fleece by the dimension of the finished felt. For example, let's say that the felted sample measured 21 centimeters ($8^1/_4$ inches). Subtract 21 centimeters ($8^1/_4$ inches) from the original 30 centimeters (12 inches) to get the change from original which is 9 centimeters ($3^1/_2$ inches). Divide the difference, 9 centimeters ($3^1/_2$ inches) by the original size, 30 centimeters (12 inches) to get the allowance for shrinkage, in this case 0.3 or 30 percent. You must allow for 30 percent shrinkage when felting with the same wool, at the same thickness, and using the same technique.

Calculating wool amounts

You'll need to know the dimension and weight of the sample and the dimension of felt needed for your project to figure out how much wool you'll need.

Let's say the sample measures 21 by 21 centimeters ($8^1/_4$ by $8^1/_4$ inches), or 441 square centimeters (68 square inches), and 28 grams (1 ounce) of wool was used. You want to make a felt jacket and for that jacket you'll need a piece of felt that measures 2 meters by 90 centimeters, or 18,000 square centimeters (79 by 36 inches, or 2844 square inches). Divide this number by the area of the sample (441 square centimeters/68 square inches) to determine how much bigger the project will be than the sample:

18,000 square centimeters ÷ 441 square centimeters (2844 square inches ÷ 68 square inches) = about 40.

So you know that the project will take about 40 times as much wool as the sample. To figure out how much this will be, multiply the weight of the wool in the sample (28 grams/1 ounce) by 40:

40 × 28 grams = about 1.1 kilogram (40 × 1 ounce = 40 ounces or $2^1/_2$ pounds) of wool.

If you want to felt two separate pieces for the jacket, for example one for the body and another for the sleeves, you'll need to determine the dimensions each piece needs to be and then use the method described above to calculate the amount of wool needed for each piece.

It can be difficult to estimate shrinkage!

Workplace

An organized workplace makes felting easier and more fun. If you felt small projects as a hobby, you can work on the kitchen counter, dining-room table, or even in the bathroom. It's best to work in an out-of-the-way room such as a bathroom or heated garage because the process can get messy.

To felt hats, socks, and other small items in the Swedish rubbing method (see page 61), use a dishpan or tray with a lip. To make large felt items with the rolling technique (see page 64), you'll need a larger work space, such as a table, covered with a heavy plastic tarp. The tarp can be dried off and stored rolled up. Holes that will inevitably appear can be repaired with duct tape. Alternatively, you can use a vinyl tablecloth or a shower curtain. Some are patterned with checks, which can be used as a grid for laying out the carded batts.

If your table is too short to accommodate the entire piece at once, try laying out some wool, wetting it, and rolling it up nearly to the end. Overlap this wet end with more dry wool and continue to lay out the wool until you get the desired length. You can also lay the fleece out on the floor.

A Waterproof Workplace

When making large wall hangings or sculpture with the rubbing technique, you will need a large work space. You can work on a large table or put together several tables of the same height. Because the rubbing technique uses quite a bit of water, the work area should have raised edges to prevent the water from running off. You can make your own raised edges by rolling up newspaper into hard rolls and taping them together with freezer tape. Tape the rolls to three edges of the table, leaving one of the short sides open. Lay a plastic tarp or shower curtain over

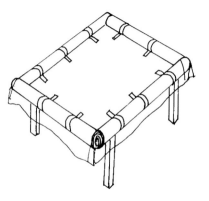

A simple, inexpensive work surface can be made by taping rolls of newspaper to a table and covering it with a plastic tarp.

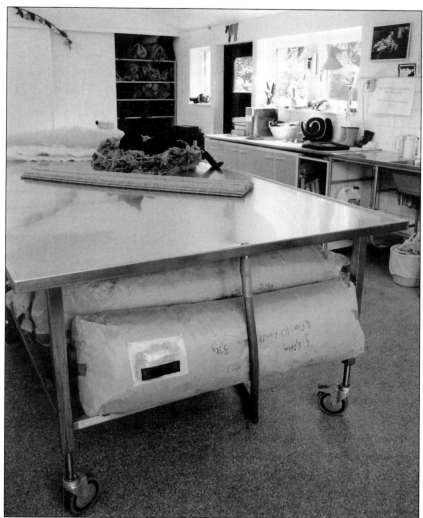

If you plan to do a lot of felting, consider purchasing a vertically adjustable table made of stainless steel that has raised edges and a hole fitted with a hose that drains to a floor drain or sink. This type of table can be ordered from companies specializing in metal fabrication (and hydraulics, if you want the table to be vertically adjustable). Carded batts and wool can be stored on the shelves under the table. Wheels on the legs make the table easy to move.

the top of the table so that the edges hang over the rolls, making sure that the tarp hangs straight down on the open side. If you wish, secure the tarp to the underside of the table with freezer tape on three sides. On the open side, place the edge of the tarp in a tub or bucket on the floor so that excess water can drain off the table while you are felting.

If you don't have a large worktable, you can use a sturdy fiberboard sheet resting on sawhorses or another table. Because leaning over can be hard on your back, use adjustable sawhorses and set them at a height that is comfortable for you. Most felters will find that kitchen counters are at a comfortable height for felting. If you plan to felt much on a fiberboard sheet, consider gluing, nailing, or securely taping two-by-twos around the edge of the board to make permanent raised edges.

Helpful Tools

Protective Equipment

Felting can cause the skin on your hands to dry and crack, especially if you work with coarse fiber and the rubbing technique. This is aggravated by washing agents, dye powders, and dye solutions. Hand protection is important; see the section on allergies (page 53).

Before washing fleece or felting, apply a generous coat of hand cream, and wear rubber gloves. For washing and dyeing, household rubber gloves are adequate. But because they are thick, you won't be able feel the fibers through them while felting. A better choice is inexpensive plastic gloves, such as those used by food handlers, which are available from drugstores. However, these extend only to the wrist. Because they do not fit snugly around the wrist, water will run into them when you use your hand to felt the inside of a project such as a hat or socks.

Surgeon's gloves are available in different sizes, fit well, are flexible, and extend halfway up the arm. Some drugstores carry surgeon's gloves, as do medical supply houses. It is well worth the investment to purchase the more expensive variety. The disposable gloves used by veterinarians are a good length and can be used repeatedly with short gloves over them.

All gloves can be reused if they are maintained well. Rinse them after each use while they are still on your hands and dry them with a towel. If the insides get wet, turn them inside out, put them back on your hands, and rinse and dry them. To make the gloves easier to pull on, sprinkle a little powder on your hands first. Apply a generous coat of hand cream after working.

Plastic or vinyl aprons are a must, and should preferably extend to below the knees. When making large, three-dimensional work such as sculpture, wear a pair of thin plastic rain pants to protect your legs. Wooden shoes tolerate puddles well!

Saponified Oil Soap

Saponified oil soap makes the felting solution alkaline (pH about 10.2 when mixed at 10 milliliters (2 teaspoons) to 1 liter (4 1/4 cups) water), which allows the fiber to swell and causes the scales to extend, making the fibers migrate more easily. In addition, saponified oil soap lubricates the individual fibers, making it easier to rub your fingers across them. Dish detergent will make the wool feel more harsh. With the rolling technique, use a little more saponified oil soap because less water is used with this technique.

You can use saponified oil soap in its liquid or solid form, and in yellow or green varieties. In southern and central

Sweden, this soap was made from hemp, which gave it a green color. In the North, animal fat was used instead, which gave the soap a yellow color. In Sweden, saponified oil soap has been available in stores since the 1800s.

Although saponified oil soap can be made from a variety of vegetable and animal fats, most that is made in Sweden contains pine oil that has been saponified with potash during heating. Pine oil is naturally yellow, so the yellow soap is not dyed. The green variety is dyed with common candy dyes. Pine oil is a by-product of the paper industry. If pine oil is not available, other natural products are used. In Denmark, for example, canola oil is used, which gives the soap a different odor and consistency. In the United States, Murphy's oil soap, which is made of saponified pine oil, is readily available. Alternatively, a gel can be made by melting 120 milliliters (1/2 cup) of grated bar soap in 3.6 liters (1 gallon) of boiling soft water.

The active ingredient in Swedish saponified oil soap is saponified pine oil. Even though saponified oil soap is environmentally friendly (it breaks down into carbon dioxide and water), it can cause an allergic reaction. Therefore, always wear gloves!

Hard Water

If your water is hard and you use saponified oil soap while felting, light lime deposits, which are impossible to remove, can form on the wool. Hard water should be softened before being used for felting. Ecover, a softener which contains zeolite and citrate, is available in Sweden. Ecover products have found there way into the United States market as well, but can be hard to find. Substitute another readily-available water softener. Washing soda, which is an environmentally friendly alternative, is unfortunately, too alkaline for wool. Other alternatives, though harsher on the environment, are tripolyphosphate and hexametaphosphate.

Felting Boards and Other Helpful Tools

To full felt with the traditional Swedish rubbing method, you'll need a felting board. Old-fashioned, galvanized, and worn washboards can be purchased cheaply in antique shops. These work well in the beginning stages of fulling, when gentle rubbing is required. But a properly effective felting board should be made of wood with milled ribs.

Hat Blocks

Hats are shaped on hat blocks. They come in different sizes or are adjustable with removable center plates.

If you have no hat block, you can substitute a variety of objects. A beach ball resting in a bowl works well. I have felted children's hats over a glass ice bucket. A pillbox hat can be felted over a small, upended plastic bucket, which will give it a sharp, neat edge. (Translator's note: There are several sources for hat blocks in the United States. Some are made of wood; others are made of polystyrene or some other poly foam material and are usually used for straw hats, but they also work for felt.)

Shoe Lasts

The best form to use for socks and boots is your own foot. If the intended recipient is not available, use a shoe last. If you're lucky, you'll find old shoe lasts at an auction or antique store. If not, you can use slabs of wood in the shape of a shoe to give you an approximate size; the felted sock or boot will take on the correct shape with use.

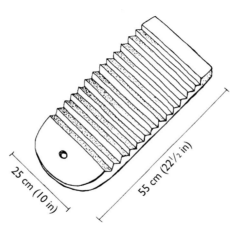

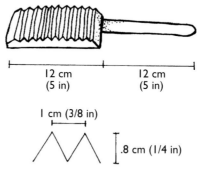

Wooden felting board. The best are made from hardwood such as birch. A simple felting board can be made by nailing three-sided ribs or common laths to a plank. You can also wind heavy rope around a plank. The board must fit down into the tub, so don't make it too wide.

12 cm (5 in)   12 cm (5 in)

1 cm (3/8 in)   .8 cm (1/4 in)

This felting tool makes the process easier on the hands. It is effective for forming hat crowns and brims, socks, and the edges of large pieces. See Sources (page 149). The tools available in the United States do not have handles.

Helpful Equipment for the Rolling Technique

When using the rolling technique to make felt (page 64), roll the wool in a supportive material that has a slightly uneven surface to create friction and facilitate felting. Below is information on some of the materials which I have tried.

Woven stick shades and bamboo mats

Window shades made of thin bamboo rods are my favorite material for rolling felt. These shades are similar to the mats made of steppe grass, *tjii*, that are used by the Torgut and other Mongolians.

The shades are easy to manage and produce fine and even felt. Roll with them out in the yard or sit in a chair. Sooner or later the cotton warp that holds the rods together will break apart, but you can repair it with thin nylon thread. Another drawback is that if the rolling is done in the sun, warp threads that cause ridges to form on the felt may not be seen but will absorb more dye than the rest of the felt. The warp threads abrade the outer layer of the wool fibers (the cuticle), causing them to take up the dye better. If the felt will not be dyed afterward, however, the stripes will never be seen.

Fabric and rolling rod

I've had good success in placing the wool on an old sheet (with the hems removed) and rolling it tightly around a metal rod that measures about 6 centimeters (2½ inches) in diameter. The tight roll can be easily worked on the floor or on a table. The rod can be stainless steel or iron that has been wrapped in plastic to protect it from rust. A heavy bar will facilitate the rolling process and hasten felting. For very thick carpets, you may want to use a thicker rod, although it may inhibit the different layers of wool from gliding past one another as easily. If you do begin with a larger rod, change to one with a smaller diameter after some of the air has been pressed out of the roll.

Of course, cloth other than sheets can be used (I've had best luck with cotton). Wash the fabric thoroughly first to eliminate any finishes that may repel water. Avoid loosely woven fabric to which the wool can adhere.

The disadvantage to these materials is that creases may form inside the roll. Open the roll often and smooth out any creases that you see. At first, the wool may adhere to the cloth, but it will loosen itself gradually. The tendency for the wool to attach to the fabric can be an advantage if you are working with design pieces. The pieces will attach to the cloth and remain correctly aligned. As the process continues, they will become fastened to the wool.

You can make as long a piece of felt as you want by overlapping the fabric and bamboo blinds as necessary. If your table is small, simply lay out as much wool and fabric as will fit and then roll them together, joining more fabric and wool as needed to get the desired length.

Plastic mats

An ordinary rug made of woven plastic strips is an excellent underlay for wool, provided you have patience. The resulting felt will be fine and uniform, but because such mats are thick, the process can take a long time. A plastic mat can prevent a felt roll from sliding when being rolled by foot on the floor. Plastic mats such as those used for sunbathing tend to be too small and slippery to be effective. They also have poor durability.

Other Equipment

Use a sprinkling bottle with fine holes or a brush dipped in a pitcher of water to sprinkle the wool. You can also use a sprinkling can or hold a colander in one hand and pour water into it from a pitcher. Move the colander around to sprinkle the water evenly over the wool.

A thick plastic tarp can be cut into pattern templates. You can make templates out of heavy fabric, but it is easier to feel the edges of a plastic template. Bubble wrap, which is used for packing, also makes good templates.

A plastic tarp or cut-open trash bags can be used to cover the worktable. Trash bags can be wrapped around the roll if you want to protect the floor you're felting on (and to keep the felt clean).

Strong rubber bands are useful for holding together the bamboo mat roll.

Plastic-coated wire, similar to twist-ties, can be used to hold a roll together when using the rolling technique. This wire is easy to twist together. It can be purchased by the spool in nurseries or hardware stores.

A bedsheet and metal bar can be used for the rolling technique. Fasten the ends of the roll with plastic-coated wire.

Felting equipment. On the left from front to back are two felting tools, hat block, wooden felting board, and galvanized washboard. In the middle is a shoe last and a mallet for hitting felt boots to full them. On the right is a stainless-steel tube, sheet, and spool of plastic-coated wire. All of the equipment sits on a woven bamboo shade, from which the large hanging rods have been removed from each end.

The Rubbing Technique

The term "rubbing technique" is used here to differentiate the traditional Nordic felting technique from the Asiatic "rolling technique". The rubbing technique is appropriate for three-dimensional items that are formed during the felting process. It also works well for pictorial works which require precise detail.

1. Lay out the first layer of wool

Hand-carded wool batts are laid out like roof shingles, overlapping one another halfway with the fibers aligned parallel to the arrow. For very thin felt, the batts can overlap just along the edge.

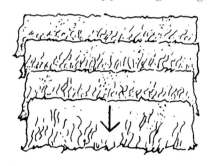

Machine-carded wool can be laid out in one thin piece, with subsequent layers aligned crosswise to previous one. Another option is to use small tufts of carded batts as the Mongolians do (see page 25).

2. Lay out the second layer of wool

Place the second layer of wool on top of and at right angles to the first as shown. You must use at least two layers of wool. Each subsequent layer is placed at right angles to the previous one.

3. Check for thin areas and add decorations

After the wool layers are laid out, feel for thin area with the use the palm of your hand. Place a thin bit of carded fleece on top of any thin areas. Add decorations such as dyed fleece, carded batts, threads, and cut-out felt pieces (see pages 68–72). If the stack of wool is thick, wet it and press out some of the air before applying the decorations so that they will stay in place better.

4. Wet the wool

Mix the felting solution as hot as your hand can stand. Use 15 to 30 milliliters (1 to 2 tablespoons) of soap gel or saponified oil soap per liter (4¼ cups) of water. The amount of soap to use depends upon the hardness of the water, cleanliness of the wool, type of wool, etc. As you pour the water, hold your hand as shown to interrupt the flow and cause the water to spread in droplets. With your palms, gently press the wool down around the edges. Push down the wool to remove the air and add more water if needed to moisten all the wool. Avoid adding too much felting solution; the wool should just be moist. If the surface is large, work the water into one small area at a time; otherwise, the water will cool down in the wool.

5. Felting

Begin by massaging the wool with very small motions. Gradually increase the pressure and range to make firm circular motions with the entire palm of your hand. Apply enough pressure to move the entire thickness of wool, not just individual fibers. To prevent stretching, always work from the outside edges in to the center. Without folding them in, work the edges with the palm of your hand to make them smooth and firm.

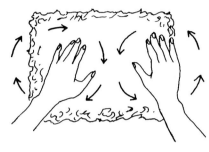

To facilitate this motion, place a very thin piece of plastic (such a dry cleaner's bag) over the wet wool, pour some felting solution on top of the plastic, and slide your fingers across the wool on top of the plastic.

6. Test for degree of felting

After working the fiber for a while, pinch it. If you can grasp single fibers, it needs more massaging. When the wool holds together in a mass, turn it over. To prevent stretching, large pieces should be rolled up before they are turned. Press out excess water and carefully hold the piece up to the light to find thin spots. (Read about how to straighten edges, layer thin spots, etc., on pages 63–64) Add fresh, hot felting solution and massage again until the other side is felted to the same hardness as the first.

7. Fulling

When both sides of the fiber hold together well, roll the mass in a piece of cotton fabric to protect it from abrasion during the fulling process. Place the felting board in a washtub to prevent spills and brace the board against your abdomen during rubbing. Rub the roll against a felting board.

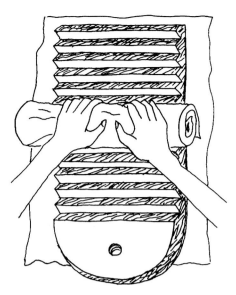

Place a damp terry-cloth towel in the tub under the felting board to help hold it steady. A galvanized metal washboard works well for the early stages of fulling. Rub the entire width of the felt at the same time. After a few minutes, unroll the felt, straighten out any wrinkles, and roll it up again from the opposite direction. Continue to full, straighten, and roll the felt from all directions.

"Dog-ears" of unfelted fleece that tend to form at the corners of the felted mass can be removed by rolling the felt diagonally from the corner to the middle. If you want the felt to have a hairy surface, remove the fabric cloth during the later stages of fulling.

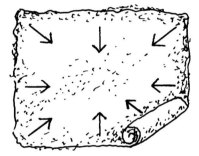

Instead of using a felting board, you can roll the cloth bundle on a table and knead it with your hands. This method works well for both large and small pictorial projects in the classroom. The fulling process can also be done in a washing machine (see page 73).

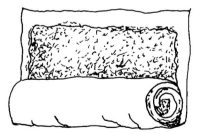

8. The fulling test

To determine if the felt is thoroughly fulled, pull on it. If it is rigid, it is finished. In some cases, a somewhat soft felt is appropriate, for example, for a tea cozy which needs to have insulating air pockets. When the quality of the felt is important, thorough fulling is necessary. Remember that shrinkage is a necessary component of fulling. If you haven't allowed for sufficient shrinkage, don't try to compensate by stopping the fulling process when the piece reaches the desired dimensions. If fulled too little, the felt will pill and become loose. It is much better to overcompensate by laying out too much fleece than too little. Washing and dyeing can cause further shrinkage of fulled fabric. You can continue to full with clean, warm water if the felt is still too loose.

Washing and other after-treatments

Finally, the felt should be washed. For different types of after-treatments, see page 79.

Shrinkage

The exact percent of shrinkage must be figured when the work needs to match a predetermined size. Measure the finished felt and see page 56 for figuring shrinkage and wool amounts.

Correcting Mistakes

Many mistakes can happen during the feltmaking process. Don't despair; most of them can be corrected!

Holes

Holes are best avoided by taking time early on to make sure that the stack of carded fleece is sufficiently thick in all areas.

Hold the felt up to the light before fulling begins. If you notice a thin area, prevent it from turning into a hole by placing a thin layer of carded fleece over the thin place (two thin layers at right angles if a hole already exists). Pour a small amount of felting solution over the fleece, cover it with a piece of thin plastic, pour a little felting solution on top of the plastic, and gently rub it. The plastic will ensure that the edges of the fleece patch will adhere to the felt.

If you find a hole after fulling has begun, rough up the surface with a steel brush so that the patch can grab onto it. If the patch still won't fasten, tack it down with sewing thread that you can remove later. If the felt is thick, you can sew on a patch with "invisible" stitches of thin, handspun thread made of the same wool as in the felt.

Holes in two-sided objects, such as hats, are repaired in the same way as described above.

Loose Flaps

Loose flaps can be carefully cut away if the wool under the flap is of an even thickness. Scratch up the clipped area with a steel brush so that it will be uneven and then rub down the loose fiber with hot felting solution. If the felt under the flap is thin, brush it up with a steel brush and felt it down into the layer beneath.

Thick Areas

Thick areas can be separated and stretched outward during the early stages of fulling. Use your hands to stretch or pull on the thick areas of felt.

Wrinkles or Folds

A wrinkle or fold of wool can develop around the edge of a template such as a hat template. It can be pulled and stretched out by firmly tugging on either side of the fold. If you cannot pull the fold apart, carefully cut the fiber in the middle of the fold. Avoid wrinkles by carefully working the wool inside and out around the edges of the template.

Design Motifs that Don't Attach

Prefelted design pieces have a better chance of attaching if you rough up the underside with a steel brush. Place a very thin bit of carded fleece on top of the surface, put the design piece on top of it, pour on hot felting solution, cover with a piece of thin plastic, pour on a little more felting solution, and rub. If just one motif will not attach, sew it down to the felt with sewing thread which can be removed after fulling is complete.

Edges

The edges of a felt piece can be made straight if early in the felting stage a thin piece of plastic is folded around the wet edge. The plastic should lie both above and below the edge and be absolutely straight with the fold of the plastic against the edge of the wool. Pour felting solution on top of the plastic and work your hands in circular motions on top of the plastic, moving toward the middle of the felt until the felt edge is tight.

Weak Edges

Weak edges in finished felt can be strengthened by sewing many stitches with thread of the same color. These threads should be invisible on the surface. Afterward, felt lightly over them with warm water. In this way, even very thin edges and points can be protected from strain.

Weak Areas

Weak areas in finished felt can be strengthened from the back side with fusible synthetic interfacing for knits. This type of facing is used for leather and can be applied with low temperatures. Afterward, it can be hidden under a facing.

You can sew on fine patches that have been felted to the exact size needed (by stretching and pulling while felted). The edges of these precisely fitting patches are finer and more durable than those cut out of felt. Because they fit the area exactly, they are nearly invisible.

Thin areas can also be strengthened from the back side with sewing thread. The thread is stitched inside the felt as if it were stuffing, but so shallow that it cannot be seen from the right side.

You can also use decorative embroidery, tambour stitchery, or hand or machine quilting to turn a mistake into a design element.

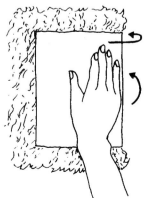

To keep the edge of the felted piece straight, fold a thin sheet of plastic around the edge of the prepared fleece.

The Rolling Technique

The rolling technique, in which wool is rolled in a mat, is a more widely used technique than the Swedish method of rubbing the wool by hand against a felting board. The rolling technique originated in Asia and Asia Minor and is used today by most felt artists and craftspeople around the world.

Large felted items such as clothing, upholstery fabric, curtains, pillows, blankets, and carpets can be made quickly and easily with the rolling technique, which is also excellent for wool that is difficult to felt. This technique is also ideal for making thin felt.

Felt made with the rolling technique has a smoother surface than that made with the rubbing technique because the peaks of the fibers are pressed together, the underside with the top side, rather than from the side toward the center. There is also less shrinkage. When processed with the rubbing method, the fibers in the felt have a chance to resume their crimp, which results in a knobby texture. If you want a thin felt with a smooth surface, you should roll the wool as the nomads do (see pages 24–25).

The following directions are for producing a thin cloth felted from two thin layers of commercially carded batts. This process requires a high degree of accuracy when the wool is laid out, so plan a small piece for your first project. If you want to use hand-carded or drum-carded wool, overlap it slightly (like the shingles on a roof) as you lay it out.

Read through the directions for the rubbing technique (page 61) and the section on equipment (page 58) before you begin. If you plan to use inlaid motifs, also read the section on motifs (pages 69–71).

1. Spread out a bamboo shade or support cloth on a table. Choose a cloth different in color from the wool you're working with so that you can see to lay out the wool evenly. The cloth should be at least 30 cm (12 inches) wider than the rolling bars.

2. Lay out the wool in at least two layers with the fibers of each layer aligned in different directions. Don't lay out the wool all the way to the edge of the support cloth. If the support cloth or bamboo shade is too short for the desired length of felt, you can join more support materials by overlapping them. This join can be made after the wool has been rolled into the first support piece if your table is small.

Begin by rolling out the carded batt. Separate off a layer of the desired thickness by putting your right hand and arm between the wool layers and carefully dividing the wool while you lift up the thin layer with your left hand. You should be able to see your hand through the layer of wool. Roll this thin layer away from the thick one in a loose roll.

Roll off another thin layer from the thick batt to prepare the bottom layer. Lay this out with the fiber perpendicular to the fibers of the previously made layer. Put the batts on the support material and thin and patch as needed.

Roll the previously made layer out on top of this one. If you are using long-fibered wool, align the fiber in the top layer perpendicular to the direction of the roll to reduce creases in the felt.

Roll out the thin batt layer on the support material, joining more support material as needed. Join the batts by slightly overlapping them and thinning out the wool in these overlapped areas. Be sure to keep the carded batts the same overall thickness.

Tear off the carded batts to the desired width. Press down hard on the edge of the batt with your left hand so that it will not stretch out as you tear.

If the wool is too thick in an area, lay your hand beside the thick area and stretch the fleece in the direction of the fibers to thin it. If any areas are too thin, lay down patches of thinned batting.

Roll the rolling bar over the batt several times to compress it and fix the joints and stretched areas. Next, roll up the batt and lay it aside. This roll will be the second layer, but is prepared first to give you a clear supporting surface to work on and to allow you to control the thickness of the bottom layer. If you were to prepare the second layer directly on top of the first, you would have trouble determining if the placement was even because the contrast between the wool and the support material would be lost.

3. Mix the felting solution, about 45 milliliters (3 tablespoons) soap gel per liter (4$\frac{1}{4}$ cups) of water. For this technique, you will need more soap in the water than is required for the rubbing technique. The water should be as hot as possible; it cools quickly. Pour the felting solution into a sprinkling bottle. You can also sprinkle the water on with a new dish brush (used ones don't produce fine enough drops), watering can, or through the holes in a colander.

4. Sprinkle the felting solution in rows over the surface so that it is applied evenly. Don't use too much solution—the surface should look as though it is slightly sweating. If the surface gets too wet, a fold will be created during rolling.

5. Lay the rolling bar on the wool and roll the support material and wool tightly together. If a crease begins to form, carefully pinch the wool and pull it up slightly, or pull on the support material to stretch out the wool. If the wool is very thick, as is required for a carpet, you can make small folds in the support material before the wool is laid out. The folds can then be stretched out as the wool is rolled up. You can also use a rolling bar with a larger diameter in the beginning of the felting process.

6. If you are using a cloth support, tie around the roll with plastic-covered wire near the ends of the roll. If using bamboo shades, secure the roll with strong rubber bands.

7. Using your forearms on a table or your feet on the floor, rotate the roll back and forth. (A plastic mat under the roll will protect your work surface.) Press down firmly and move your arms or feet over the whole roll so that it all receives the same amount of friction. If there are several people rolling at once, change places after a while to ensure that the rolling is even. Turn the roll over every so often so that all of the sides will eventually roll against the table or floor.

Continue to roll for about 5 minutes. Open the roll and see if is possible to loosen the felt from the support material. If the felt does not adhere to the support material, it must be rolled longer. If it sticks so well to the support material that it is difficult to loosen, it has been rolled too long. If the felt will not come loose, roll some more, and eventually it should shrink itself loose.

Loosen the felt from the cloth and stretch out any creases. Lay fleece patches on any thin areas. This is the time to incorporate design motifs. Lay the motifs on the felt, and adjust and stretch them as needed.

Sprinkle more felting solution over the entire surface. Folds are less likely to form by the addition of too much moisture now than during the initial wetting. This time, roll the packet from the opposite end, stretching the support material and felt as you roll.

8. Roll for about 10 minutes. Then open the roll and check the thickness and pattern. In areas where the felt is unacceptably thin, roughen up the surface of the felt with a steel-bristled brush, add more wool, and sprinkle with felting solution.

Roll up the packet again, this time in the original direction.

9. Roll the packet for 10 to 15 minutes, unroll, and check the density of the felt. Repeat this step until you're satisfied with the density. With each repeat, turn the felt over and roll it from the opposite end, stretching it as you roll. After the felt has been turned several times, make sure that the pattern side is facing up so that the design motifs will be on the inner curve of the roll. This will make the right side of the felt smoother than the back side.

Sprinkle the felt with hot felting solution as needed; the felt should be moist, but not dripping wet. You can roll the felt anywhere. To protect carpets and floors from moisture, place the roll inside a plastic trash bag, twist the ends together, bind them with twist-ties, and cover the seal with tape.

It is important that the felt be kept warm. This can be done with hot felting solution or by steaming, which keeps the wool at the right temperature and conserves the solution.

10. Continue rolling the felt until it is at or near the desired hardness and then knead the wool with a little warm felting solution. This gives the felt a more textured surface and is quicker than rolling.

You can also alternate between rolling and kneading. If you end with rolling, the felt will be smoother than if you end with kneading. The goal in this process is to achieve firm, solid felt. If it is too loose, the felt will become nappy, and garments made from it will lose their shape quickly.

Fulling can also be done in a washing machine (see page 73). With this method, the felt will be more porous, tough, and nubby. The wool must be well felted before it can be put into the machine for fulling.

The entire felting process need not be completed in one day. Unfinished felt can be left rolled up and moist for a couple of days. If the work must wait longer, unroll the felt and let it dry. When you return to the work, sprinkle the felt with fresh felting solution. But don't wait more than a few days before completing the work; the alkaline felting solution will cause the wool to deteriorate if left too long. *(Translator's note: You can rinse out the felting solution, let the piece dry, and then return to it at a much later date.)*

Never allow dirty wool to lie in a roll for any period of time. The dirt can sink to the bottom of the roll and form small gray stripes on the surface that will not wash out.

See pages 43 and 79 for washing instructions and after-treatments.

To make many felt pieces the same thickness, weigh equal amounts of wool and lay it out in the same configuration for each piece.

Forget aerobic classes and make felt with your whole body instead! Here, the rolling is being done between the hands, beneath the feet, and under the bottom at the same time.

Felting Designs

Patterned felt can look like almost anything you want.

It can look like a watercolor painting with colors that imperceptibly shift over one another.

It can look like a printed cloth with motifs that have sharp and clear contours.

It can look like glass art with a design that lies mysteriously hidden under a translucent layer.

It can look like stone, moss, or lava with an organic surface structure.

It can look like woven cloth with a distinct thread structure.

The possibilities are endless!

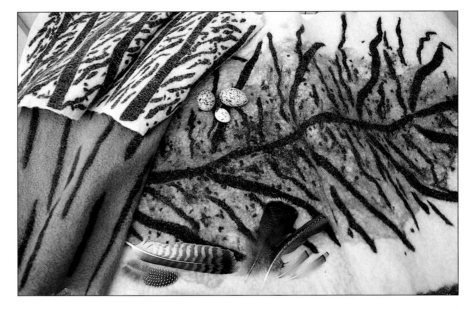

Sample first

Always make several samples before tackling a large project. During felting, designs change substantially; some effects may disappear into the background wool, the colors may blend in unexpected ways, fibers may migrate, and shapes may transform. Remember to allow for shrinkage (30 to 50 percent) when planning your designs.

Color Changes

The color of the background wool affects the overall color in the finished felt. A white background will make colors appear pastel. Gray will dull colors. Black will dim colors, but also frame them so that they shine. Colors blend during felting just as watercolors blend in painting. The thicker the design piece, the more of its own color it will hold.

It is important to rinse out all excess dye from the wool used for the design pieces. Otherwise, the dye may bleed onto the background wool during felting, moth-proofing, or washing.

Technical Tips

Motifs can be made in many different ways. They can be made of uncarded or carded wool, felt, yarn, cloth, grass, sticks, or other material.

The best way to felt in a design is to lay it upside down and mirror-imaged onto the bamboo mat or cloth and then lay the background wool on top of it. This helps the design stay in place during rolling; if the design is placed on top of the background wool, it is more likely to shift when rolled. The thicker and more numerous the layers, the greater the risk of shifting. Sometimes, however, you may want to see the design from the right side, on top of the background, to decide where to place it and evaluate how the colors look together. To do this, lay out the background wool, sprinkle it lightly with felting solution, and roll it for five minutes to press out most of the air and compress the wool. If the surface of the wool is very smooth, use a steel-bristled brush to roughen the areas where the design motifs will be placed. After positioning the design motifs, carefully roll the whole unit together and roll it for two minutes. Then unroll the felt and check the position of the motifs. If the pattern pieces do not adhere to the background felt, brush the back of the pattern pieces and the surface of the background felt again with the steel-bristled brush.

If you have laid out a mirror-imaged pattern under the background wool, remember to turn the felt over so that it is right side up during the last stages of felting. Being on the inner curve of the roll will give the right side a smoother surface.

Troubleshooting

If the pattern doesn't attach to the background felt and you are in the beginning of the felting process, you have not worked long enough. Continue rolling.

If the felt used for the pattern motif has been fulled too much, there will be no surface fibers to grab onto the background wool. Rough up both the background wool and the back of the motif with a steel-bristled brush. If you are working with large shapes that will not attach, sew them down with a few basting stitches and remove the thread when the felt is finished.

If the background is Rya (or other long, coarse wool) that has been machine-carded, there may be too few fiber ends sticking up from the ground to grab onto the pattern pieces. Such long fibers may adhere to each other and may not stick up enough for other fibers to adhere to them. This problem must be resolved when the layer to which the design will adhere is laid out. Tear off a small tuft of carded batt and use your right hand to hold the tuft down on the surface of the background felt. With your left hand, press down on the wool that is sticking out from under your right hand, and then pull the loose fleece away with your right hand. Repeat this process until the surface is filled with wool tufts.

Motifs of Uncarded Wool

In its natural state, raw wool can be an inspiration. I keep a collection of pretty pieces of different fleeces that can be used for decoration. Some fleeces have beautiful color, lovely structure, or extraordinary luster, all of which keep me from carding apart its splendor!

Choose a pretty wool staple and divide it into clumps or pull at its sides to spread it out. Lay it on the background wool in a pleasing arrangement. If the staple contains long, shiny outercoat fibers, lay a small amount of the carded background fiber on top of them to help hold them down. Pull four or five fibers out of the carded wool and lay them over the wispy points of staple.

Motifs of Cut Pieces of Felt

Motifs cut out of felt work well in designs that have repeated elements. Using a pattern, it is easy to cut out several shapes and lay them out on the surface.

It is best to lay out the pattern upside down and mirror-imaged.

Tips on designing

1. Cut out geometric shapes such as circles, ovals, or squares from colored paper. Lay these shapes on paper that is the same color as the background felt. Move the shapes around and evaluate the possibilities. Is there too much color? Are some of the colors weaker than others? Do they fall out of the design? Are the motifs too near to or too far from one another? Is the design balanced?

2. Create designs from objects found in nature. Shapes of animals, insects, and fish can make beautiful motifs. The strata of stones and the patterns on their surface posess interesting color and shape combinations. Try to imagine how the motif will look over the entire piece, whether it be a garment, wall hanging, or pillow. Draw a design and modify it before working with the wool.

3. Common, simple everyday objects can inspire a design. Candy, buttons, thread spools, pens, cars, boats—the possibilities are endless. Remember, the shape should not be complicated if you plan to cut out dozens of pieces!

The felt used for the pattern motifs should be porous and only lightly felted if it is to attach to the background wool. Use the rolling technique to make the felt for motifs, but roll it only a few times. If the motif felt is fulled too much, rough up the back of the motif with a steel-bristled brush so that it will adhere to the background felt.

You can make the motif felt out of dyed batts, or you can dye the wool after felting. If you want to dye after felting, felt lightly. The wool will continue to shrink when the felting solution is washed out of it and when it is dyed.

The rigidity of the motif felt affects the pattern's appearance. Loosely felted, soft motif felt will produce a sunken-in shape with soft, undefined edges, whereas tightly felted, hard motif felt will produce a sharper image that will stand out on top of the surface.

The thickness of the motif felt will also affect the pattern's appearance. A thick motif felt gives the design clear color, whereas thin felt will blend with the color of the background wool and appear unclear and mottled.

The type of wool used for the motif felt is also a factor. Coarse fiber will produce an unclear contour; fine fiber will produce a sharp one. A pattern of Rya wool on a fine-wool background will produce a design that "swells" because Rya wool shrinks considerably less than does fine wool. In general, the cut felt motifs will shrink less than the background wool because the wool in the motifs has already experienced some shrinkage during initial felting.

Motifs Under the Felt Surface

Subtle, barely discernible patterns in bas-relief can be achieved by using cut pieces of thick, well-fulled felt. Lay them on the background wool, cover them with the thinnest batt that you can manage, and roll it all together. You can lay threads, cloth pieces, and other materials between carded batts in this way. If you sandwich a motif between two thin batts, the felt will be almost transparent and the motif will stand out.

Motifs Made of Carded Wool

Traditionally, simple felt carpets, such as the *tekemet* carpets made by the Kazakhs and the *alakiiz* carpets made by the Kirghiz, had designs made of carded, unfelted wool. The design elements in these carpets—borders and large shapes—would be difficult, if not impossible, to create with motifs cut from felt.

However, a large patterned surface of carded wool takes time and requires great skill if the design is to be distinct. With good skill and fine fiber, a design of carded wool can be made as sharp and distinct as one made with cut shapes.

Use carded wool designs to get special effects, such as indistinct or nearly invisible color transitions. Carded wool can be used to create an effect similar to that of painting with a brush.

Inspiration

Study old rustic utilitarian items at a museum. Choose a composition with simple lines and large pattern shapes. Sketch the pattern and then adapt it for a felt carpet, seat pad, or other article. Simplify and change the motif so that it will fit into your format. Eliminate elements that you don't find visually pleasing.

To lay out the design, use a piece of

The design is drawn with tailor's chalk or with dampened pencil roving. Carded wool is laid out in torn-off tufts.

The design for this surface is made of dyed carded wool.

cloth as a support material. Dampen the cloth and draw the pattern onto it with a tailor's pencil. Cover the drawn shapes with carded wool in the following way.

1. Lay out whole pieces of batt in crossing layers and tear them off along the edge of the drawn shape. Layer thickly if you want bold color and thinly if you want the background color to show through. For clean, sharp edges, fold in the wispy fiber that sticks out around the edges of the drawn shape. Sprinkle a little water on the edges and press them into the background wool.

2. Tear off small tufts of carded batt by taking a piece of the batt in your right hand and laying this hand against the surface of the support material. With the left hand, press down on the fleece that sticks out from under the right and pull the right hand away. The loose fleece will come away with the right hand.

Repeat this step, laying the fibers of the next tuft perpendicular to the previous one until the drawn shape is filled with fleece tufts. For clean, sharp edges, fold in the fiber wisps that stick out around the edges. Sprinkle a little water on the edges and press them down into the background wool.

Small shapes and lines are easiest to render if the fleece is dampened before it is formed into a shape. The dampness helps the piece stay in place. Lines will be cleaner and sharper if they are made from twisted strings of wet batting (such as pencil roving). You can also spin a

loose thread on a spindle or use commercial pencil roving. If your design has a lot of thin lines, it is best to use commercial pencil roving or a barely spun yarn such as Lopi.

Movable Shapes Made of Carded Wool

Stable shapes, which you can easily move around from one position to another, can be made by dampening wool, silk, flax, yarn, or some other material with wallpaper paste and then forming it to the desired shape, using plastic as a work surface. (*Translator's note: If you have difficulty finding wallpaper paste, you can substitute soluble methylcellulose, which is available from art supply stores and stores that supply paper makers.*) This method is ideal for complicated shapes. When the paste has dried, the rigid shape can be loosened from the plastic and positioned on the background wool. The paste will dissolve during felting.

The Dutch artist Inge Evers developed the following technique for felting silk shapes: Lay out a piece of synthetic marquisette, bridal tulle, no-see-ums insect netting, or other fine net material that is twice the size of your design motifs. Pull out small, cloudlike wads of silk fiber and gently drop them onto one half of the netting in the desired pattern. Fold

the other half of the netting over the silk fiber. Dip a sponge into wallpaper paste that has been mixed to the consistency of yogurt, and wet the silk fiber evenly. Soak up any excess paste with a clean sponge. Lift the net with the enclosed silk and hang it to dry. Peel off the net and cut the desired shapes out of the glued silk, or felt the whole thing as it is. (*Translator's note: Carol Beadle developed this same technique in Berkeley in the early 1970s. It is a case of parallel development, each artist independently working on the same technique.*)

Dyed, Carded Fleece Used as the Design for the Whole Cloth

Composition Tips

To plan and visualize multicolored felt, try painting with watercolors. Wet a large sheet of watercolor paper and then, with clean colors in your brush, paint with rhythmic strokes, letting the colors mix and blend on the paper. Try painting lines, squares, speckles, and waves. Paint many papers using different colors, brush strokes, and patterns. With plain white paper, cut a stencil in the shape of the felt piece you are planning. Choose a part of the painted paper you find interesting and place the stencil over it. The white paper will frame that section and block off the rest so that you can get an idea of how the colors will look in the felt project. Dye carded fleece the same colors that you painted with.

Lay out the dyed, carded fleece over the background wool in the same way that you painted with the watercolors, laying the dominant color on top. Use many thin sheets of carded batts and let the colors blend in overlapping layers.

Designs Made From Yarns, Threads, Flax, Silk, and Other Materials

To make straight lines in a design, use porous, loosely spun yarn. The yarn should be unplied and of the pencil roving type (tightly plied yarn will not shrink into a straight line but will make small waves in the finished felt). Use yarn of fine undercoat wool; long, coarse fibers of the outercoat will have a wavy appearance.

Yarn can be laid out in squares, lines, and spirals, or in total disarray. Long flax fibers (line) can be pulled out at the sides to create a fine mesh. Flax and silk reflect light and can add an interesting contrast to the matte felt, which absorbs nearly all light.

Long-fibered or shiny material may be difficult to attach to the ground wool. When using this type of fiber, lay a very thin layer of carded fleece over it to help hold it in place.

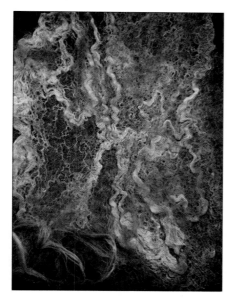

Inlaid flax fiber.

Smocking and Cloqué

This technique works well with loosely woven, open cloth such as sackcloth, linen, silk chiffon, silk or synthetic organza, gauze, or thin Lurex.

Smocking can be done with soft synthetic or silk organza. Because the quality of the cloth is essential to the success of the technique, experiment with small pieces of cloth before purchasing enough for a large project. Lay two thin layers of carded batt on the background wool and cover them with organza. Roll until the cloth and the wool join. Because the wool will shrink during rolling and the cloth will not, the cloth will form bubbles on the surface of the wool. Rolling in one direction only will make "smocking" folds form.

A stiff organza used in this way will form bubbles instead of folds, and is called wool cloqué.

Wool smocking with inlaid synthetic organza.

Wool cloqué with inlaid synthetic organza. Clothing in the same material is shown on page 97.

Stockholmsvägen 92. Gunilla Paetau Sjöberg. Different techniques are combined in one picture. Inlaid carded batts and uncarded wool form the background. The house is embroidered and appliquéd, and the foreground bushes are inlaid felt pieces.

Embroidered text can be sewn freehand or over drawn outlines.

Text can be cut out of felt or laid out in rainbow-dyed silk or moist drawn-out fiber from a carded batt. Use the method for laying out as described for designs with the right side facing up (see page 70). Form movable letters of carded fleece by wetting the fleece with wallpaper paste and allowing it to dry before cutting the letters out (see page 70).

A "Genuine" Mock Pelt

A mock pelt made of shorn fleece can be made by taking several wool staples at a time, drawing them out slightly to the side at the root ends, and laying them down in rows with the roots aligned in the same direction on carded batts or, preferably, on lightly felted wool. The wool staples should be laid out so that each row covers the root half of the previous row. The undercoat in the staple will attach to the carded batts while the tip of the staple and the longer outercoat hair will lie free.

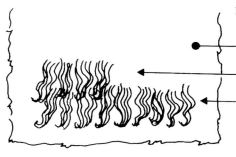

Fleece layout for "genuine" mock pelt.

— Carded batt

2. Lay out row 2 with wool staples.

1. Lay out row 1 with wool staples.

Felting with Machines

In reading old Swedish chronicles about felt, I've come across the word "filta". According to Swedish dictionaries from the Middle Ages, the word "filta" has two meanings: "arduous work" and "to fight". Can it be that the old felting technique was such arduous work it was dubbed "filta"? Or did the ancients have to "fight" with the wool to make the incredibly hard and strong felt, resistant to both fire and iron weapons, as reported by historians? Contemporary hand-workers specializing in felt shoes and boots beat the wool with wooden mallets and bats to make the necessary hard felt.

Feltmaking is still arduous labor for handworkers, though they no longer make shields for use in war. Feltmakers have long tried to minimize this effort. Katarina Ågren reports how the Östman family in Svedjeholmen, Ångermanland, adapted a cream separator for felting work before the 1920s.

Unfortunately, most of us do not have access to camels and horses, but we do have bicycles! Why not drag a felt roll behind your bicycle when going back and forth to the post office? I have heard about an American who invented "auto felt" by dragging a roll behind her car as she drove around a large parking lot.

Felt while you cycle! Here is a simple felting machine constructed of stainless-steel tubing. Inside the tubing is a somewhat longer vinyl pipe, and inside the pipe is a soft wire. A stick holds the wire out so that the rods can roll. The roll is covered by a strong tarp. Pictured here is a triple construction, but it is much more difficult to handle than a single tube.

Washing Machine

Perhaps a washing machine offers the easiest mechanization. Use a washing machine that can be opened at any stage of the cycle so that the fulling progress can be monitored. Top-loading machines are the easiest to use.

If you have the space and resources, install a washing machine to be used exclusively for the fulling of felt to eliminate the inevitable collection of hair on your clothes. Because the machine need only have a functioning motor, look for a cheap used machine. As a rule, the heating element of a washer is the first to break, so many basements and garages harbor otherwise useless machines that would work fine for felting.

Fulling Yardage

Felt that has been fulled in a washing machine has a different character than felt that has been rolled. The former is more porous, thick, shaggy, and knobby. It is suitable for winter jackets.

Begin by laying out the wool on a bamboo mat or on a sheet as you would for the rolling method (see page 64). Lay the wool out more thinly than you normally would. It will shrink quite a bit more if it is fulled in the machine than if the rolling technique is used exclusively. Roll the wool until it is thoroughly felted—if the felting stage is not complete, the wool may shrink too much during machine fulling and could end up shaggy and thick. It isn't a problem if the wool has become attached to the support cloth, in fact, it is an advantage. The cloth will stabilize the wool and reduce shrinkage during machine fulling. When the cloth begins to form large bubbles on the surface of the felt, separate the two, and then full the felt alone a little longer.

Fill the machine to about one-fourth the height of the drum with water at about 45°C (113°F). If the wool has not been washed, add a gentle laundry detergent that contains no bleach. If you use saponified oil soap, add only a very small amount. Clean wool requires no fulling agent. Place the felt in the machine.

After about five minutes of the wash cycle, stop the machine, open the lid, and check the felt. Continue this way, stopping the machine and checking the felt every few minutes until the felt is the quality you want. This can happen very quickly, so check it often. If the wool is dirty, spin out the wash water and refill to half of the drum height with fresh lukewarm water for rinsing. Let the machine run for a few minutes, drain, spin out, and add more clean rinse water. If the fulling is finished before the last rinsing, rinse the felt by hand in a bucket or bathtub. My machine has a delicate cycle that allows all of the needed rinsings before the fulling is finished.

Felting three-dimensional shapes

Balls, figures, and other sculptural objects such as socks can be felted and fulled entirely or partially in the washing machine. I have the best luck with round shapes—they keep their shape when they hit against the drum of the machine. Irregular shapes can be problematic.

For this type of washing-machine fulling you will need old panty hose and plastic-covered wire to tie the hose. The hose should be fine and tight; open and loosely woven hose will attach to the wool. Cut off the pants part and just use the legs. Fine-mesh washing bags can also be used.

Balls and other compact shapes

Balls and other compact shapes can be made entirely of wool or can be built around a core of foam rubber. Prepare the ball as described on page 82 up to the point where the felting begins. Don't be stingy with the wool if you use a foam-rubber core. Wool shrinks a lot in the washing machine and if it is not thick enough, it may leave holes through which the foam rubber may show.

Push the object down to the bottom of the stocking. Tighten the stocking around it and tie it off with a piece of plastic-covered wire. If you have multiple objects, push the next one down into the stocking and tie it off with plastic-covered wire. Continue in this manner until the stocking is filled.

Irregular shapes that have protruding parts are more difficult to handle. The protrusions can become rounded and obscured during felting. Therefore, when cutting foam rubber shapes to be covered with felt, exaggerate the details; for instance, lengthen a pointed nose. Carefully wind carded fleece around the foam rubber. Wind the fiber in different directions. Cut the stockings into long bandagelike units, about 6 cm (2½ inches) wide. Wind these strips around the fleece-covered shape. Secure the end of the wrapped stocking with a safety pin. (Remove the pin immediately after fulling; otherwise, it will rust.)

Follow the instructions on page 73 for fulling fabric in the machine. Let the shapes agitate no longer than three minutes. Pull out a shape, take off the stocking and check the progress. If the wool has formed a tight skin, the stocking can be removed. Although the wool shell

may seem loose over the foam rubber, the fibers should have felted to one another. As soon as the shell has formed, remove the stockings and put the shapes back into the machine. If the stockings stay on too long, the wool will attach to them. Because all machines have different degrees of agitation, make a sample with one ball or shape before you begin mass production.

Of course, you can felt the objects by hand first and just do the fulling in the machine.

Fulling felt socks and other hollow objects

Hard-fulled, hollow objects that will be stuffed later can also be fulled in the machine after having been felted by hand to the point at which the felt holds together well. You will have the best luck with shapes that are regular and round. Protruding shapes can be obscured during felting; for example, the toes of socks and boots can become blunted.

Put a template of light but firm material inside an irregular shape. I don't recommend using wooden lasts for this purpose—they are hard on the machine and the ears! Extra-hard foam rubber makes a good template; soft foam rubber will collapse during fulling. You can glue pieces of foam rubber together to get the needed shape. Using a ballpoint pen, draw the shape on the foam rubber a few centimeters (an inch or so) larger than the size of the finished object. With a sharp knife, carve the foam rubber into a crude shape and then fine-tune it with scissors or an electric knife. To ensure that the foam-rubber template will hold the form of a sock or boot, place a purchased, very hard felt sole under the foam-rubber foot. Then put the foam-rubber foot and felt sole into a plastic bag and tape over all of the folds and openings with waterproof plastic tape. Put this foot form inside the wool sock or boot and put the whole thing in the machine. Because the cuff and instep are difficult to full in the machine, give these parts an extra round of fulling afterward with a hand-held felting tool (see page 59).

The apples in this wall hanging by Gunilla Paetau Sjöberg were felted in the washing machine.

A nylon stocking is excellent for felting balls in the washing machine. Tie it with plastic-coated wire.

Sanders

Some feltmakers have experimented with a finishing or orbital sander. Brita Jacobsson, Surahammar, Sweden, has good success using a sander for three-dimensional felting. Her knees, back, and arms have caught up with her seventy years, and the sander brings welcome relief from the strenuous work. A sander is ideal for small pieces.

To felt with a sander, moisten the wool with felting solution in the usual way. Push out the air and use a towel to sop up any extra water. You can work directly on the wool or on top of a thin plastic sheet that covers the wool. The plastic prevents water from getting into the sander. Use the sander with the sanding plate attached, but without sandpaper. "Sand" the wool in small areas of overlapping squares. When the wool fibers are attached to each other, the sander can be glided over the entire piece. Brita often finishes her pieces with a bit of ordinary rolling.

Brita Jacobsson felting with a sander.

Take care when working with motors in a moist environment. Even if the motor is well shielded in the machine, keep your hands dry and don't let water sprinkle into the motor.

Brita's skillful husband has built a little felting machine out of a sander and the polishing adapter from a vacuum cleaner. Although the machine looks promising, such a vibrating machine can cause blood-vessel, nerve, and muscle damage over time and with intensive use.

Little Red Riding Hood and the Wolf by Brita Jacobsson. Brita specializes in illustrating stories and folktales. She makes extraordinary small figures and detailed environments and often assembles them in deep, glass covered, wooden frames. She sometimes sews together small pieces of felt and models the figures with needle and thread. Her small stitches, which are either hidden in the wool or visible for effect, are repeated over and over until the image is correct.

Felting Machines

I saw the work of Jenny Kyle at an exhibition in Sweden where her traditional, yet playful work filled two rooms. She mixed animal motifs with geometric shapes, particularly triangles.

Jenny, who comes from Devon, England, explained that she felted and fulled with the help of a felting machine that she and her husband, Doug, had built. Her work is very smooth and fine. Plans for a similar felting machine are on page 77. If you construct your own machine, do so at your own risk. Keep the machine in a safe place, away from children and other inexperienced users. Be sure to shield the motor and circuit breaker from water.

Jenny's machine measures about 1.25 by 2.5 meters (4 by 8¹/₄ feet). It consists of a sturdy metal frame with a bottom plate upon which rows of plastic pipes are placed. The felt is placed between two sheets of wood on top of the pipes. The motor sits on one end of bottom sheet and makes it move slightly back and forth. The upper sheet is a lid that can be placed on or removed from the felt surface with the help of a rope and pulley in the ceiling.

The strong metal frame is welded together with angle and plate iron and stands on the floor on short iron legs.

A base made of 18-millimeter (3/4-inch) plywood is held within the metal frame. Resting on this base are a number of plastic pipes, followed by another 18-millimeter (3/4-inch) plywood sheet to which the motor is attached. This is the sheet that moves back and forth.

The lid is made of 12-millimeter (1/2-inch) plywood. It can be lifted up and down with a rope and pulley that is attached to the ceiling. During felting, a small weight is placed on top of the lid to keep it snug against the felt to create friction.

Plans for a Felting Machine

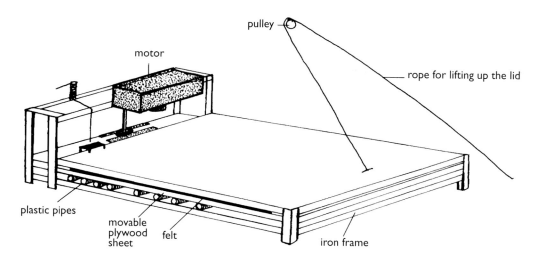

pulley

rope for lifting up the lid

motor

plastic pipes

movable
plywood
sheet

felt

iron frame

Side view

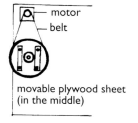

gear

lid

felt

plastic pipes

bottom plate firmly
assembled in the iron
frame

movable plywood
sheet

Machine from Above

motor

belt

movable plywood sheet
(in the middle)

Detail of the iron frame construction from
the side

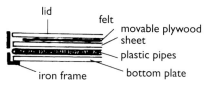

lid

felt

movable plywood
sheet

plastic pipes

iron frame

bottom plate

Jenny and Doug Kyle with a machine-felted
hanging.

Jenny Kyle with her felting machine

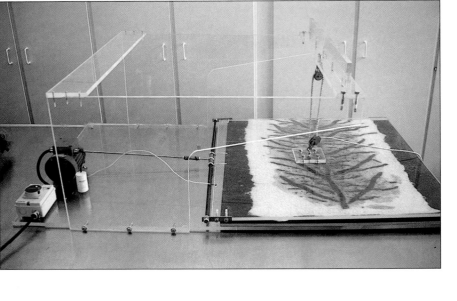

A felting machine that I adapted from an idea of American felter **Larry Beede**. The original plywood sheet has been replaced with acrylic, which holds up better when wet. Instead of using a block and tackle in the ceiling to lift the upper sheet, an super structure is used, which makes the machine portable. Large items can be felted by laying the wool between pieces of cloth for support and then moving them around by hand.

The basic plan for the modified Larry Beede felting machine.

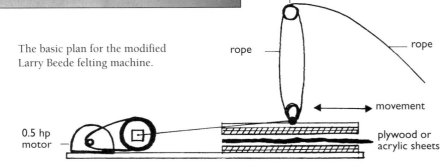

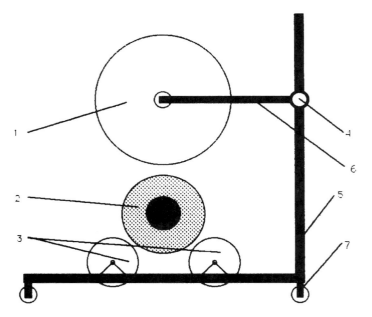

Felt machine constructed by Americans **Phillip Baldwin** and **Layne Goldsmith**. The dampened wool is rolled between bamboo mats around a foam-rubber core and tied as in traditional feltmaking. The felt roll is then placed on the drive rollers, the machine is turned on, and the pressure-roller boom is lowered onto the felt. With the use of a block and tackle, the boom can be lowered to exert more pressure or raised slightly to put less pressure on the felt roll. Hot water and felting solution can be added to hasten the process. After about 20 to 40 minutes of rolling, the pressure boom is raised, and the roll is removed and unrolled. The felt is then rolled from a different direction and the process repeated. The maximum width of the felt is about 3 meters (10 feet); the length capacity has not yet been determined.

1. Pressure roller, diameter 30 cm (12 in)
2. Felt roll with foam-rubber core
3. Drive roller, diameter 11.5 cm ($4^1/2$ in), 45 rpm
4. Pressure roller boom hinge
5. Welded metal frame, square tube
6. Pressure-roller boom
7. Wheel-mount socket

The Fulling Methods

Felt that is fulled on a felting board shrinks considerably both in width and length because it is pushed from all sides when it is rubbed. The fibers also have a chance to regain their natural crimp, which causes a bumpy surface. If you use a wooden felting board, the resulting felt surface will be somewhat hairy, especially if the ribs are deep and far apart.

The smoothest surface and thinnest felt is created when the felt is fulled by rolling either around a bar or inside a bamboo mat. If it is worked long enough, this rolling method will also make the most compact felt. With this method, the felt is not pressed in from the sides, and the top is pressed along with the underside, making very thin felt. This method also causes less shrinkage.

Felt which is fulled in the washing machine shrinks more in both width and length, is more porous, leathery, and elastic, and is bumpier on the surface. The outercoat of long-fibered wool such as Rya can make shiny loops on the surface. This can be an advantage or disadvantage, depending on the effect you desire.

Think about the characteristics of the felt that you want to create and choose the fulling method accordingly.

After-Treatments

When the felt item has been washed and spun out, block it into shape by pulling and tugging on its edges. Smooth the piece out and then drape it over a log or similar large, round object. Don't hang it over a clothesline: the thin line will cause ridges.

With these simple treatments, the felt will be flat but will retain its bumpy texture.

Pressing

Pressing with a hot iron over a moist cloth will lightly compress the felt and stabilize it. Repeated pressing will help to make a shape more firm.

Mangling

Mangling gives the surface of felt a very smooth and shiny appearance, which is appropriate for clothing. The felt must be damp, but can be either cold or warm when mangled. If you have processed the felt in a washing machine, mangle just after the rinse water is spun out. If you are not using a spinner, let the water drain from the cloth and then place it on newspapers to absorb excess water. Mangle the felt when it is lightly and evenly moist.

If you use a small table mangle, avoid letting fibers accumulate around the cylinders. I mangle long pieces of felt in two rounds. I first roll in half of the cloth from one end and let it sit in the mangle for several hours. Then I roll in the other half of the cloth from the other end and let it remain in the mangle. This procedure is easier and more effective than pressing. When using a small mangle, you may have to fold the felt in half to fit it between the rollers. The crease can be pressed out later.

Brushing

To produce a surface that is soft and warm, perhaps for the inside of a sock, mitten, or sleeping bag, brush up the nap of the felt to make it loftier and warmer. Brushing will also make a prickly fabric feel smoother. The ends of short, hard outercoat hair can be itchy if they stick out of the felt. When brushed, they will become a little longer and will lie over the surface rather than stick out of it.

Brush felt with a steel-bristled brush when it is still moist. Brush away from you in a single direction, beginning at the edge closest to you.

Sizing, Strengthening, and Stiffening

You may find that you want to make a three-dimensional form such as a hat or a bowl very stiff or maybe strengthen a small sculpture or part of a large textile. You may want to strengthen the parts of a hat which do not hold their shape well in use, for example, the brim's outer edge. In some cases, the decorations on a surface need to be strengthened to hold their shape.

The first time I needed to stiffen a surface decoration was when I made a felt picture which included a three-dimensional snail. I wanted the five tentacles to stand out of the background but to be made of fiber. Glue and common textile stiffeners didn't allow the wool points to keep the look of fiber. I then tried Hungarian mustache wax with excellent results!

But mustache wax is not suitable for everything. For large objects, use the special stiffener for felt hats called *sizing*. Sizing is painted on the inside of the felt with a brush or a piece of sponge. The stiffener can be diluted with thinner to produce a slightly more flexible felt. Hat sizing adds a light film to the felt surface, which can make it somewhat lighter in color. *(Translator's note: Spray sizing is available from millinery supply companies in the United States.)*

You can make classic hatmakers' sizing from *shellac flakes*. Shellac is a resin-like secretion from an insect. Shellac comes in many colors. The lightest, white shellac, is the most expensive. Lemon yellow and orange varieties cost two-thirds as much as the white. The lemon yellow variety turns light brown when painted onto white felt, so it is best to use it on a dark felt.

Shellac flakes can be dissolved in denatured alcohol. Working in a well-ventilated area and wearing a mask, mix one part shellac with five parts alcohol in a container with a tight-fitting lid. Let it stand, covered, for two to three days, or until the flakes are dissolved in the alcohol. The sizing soaks into the felt without affecting the hairy surface. When the alcohol evaporates, the shellac is left as small crystals. This sizing can withstand careful washing; lift the felt up and down in the washing bath and do not crumple it.

Shellac can also be purchased in solution form in paint stores, but this concentration gives a very hard surface. It must be diluted with denatured alcohol. It is usually available only in brown color. *(Translator's note: Shellac solutions in the United States are available at paint stores in clear and orange varieties.)*

Paint stores carry many different types of varnish which may also work. A durable possibility is *alkyd wood varnish,* in a satin (semimatte) finish, such as the type used for interior woodwork. Paint the varnish on the back side of a hat or on the right side of a sculpture, using a small, flat brush. If a softer quality is desired, add lacquer thinner (naphtha-lene). This varnish won't change the color of the felt.

Another alternative is interior *acrylic/polyurethane varnish* which can be diluted with water. Apply the diluted varnish in successive layers until the desired degree of hardness is achieved. The varnish creates a thin film which makes the felt slightly lighter in color.

Another, somewhat more expensive alternative is *acrylic varnish*. The brand that I tested can be diluted with water. It gave a slightly stronger sheen to the flat surface of the felt than any of the previously named options.

In summary, nearly all of the acrylic/polyurethane or acrylic varnishes give a hard and slightly noticeable surface, even hat sizing. However, the alkyd wood varnish is the least visible on the felt surface, and it gives just the right degree of hardness in its pure state.

Sculpture and Relief

Three-dimensional items make good use of the unique characteristics of felt. While other textiles make fine sculpture, felted wool is especially suited for the task. Felt sculptures can be made in a variety of ways.

Solid, Compact Shapes

Solid, compact shapes made entirely of wool are easy and fun to make. You can felt layer upon layer of carded wool by hand, creating any kind of irregular shape. You are restricted only by the weight of the final piece: thick wool can be prohibitively heavy.

The tentacles on this snail were stiffened with mustache wax.

When sculpting, use at least twice the amount of felting solution that you would normally use. To facilitate the process, add a few drops of soap to your hands.

A shape can also be formed by carving and cutting into a block of felted wool with a sharp knife. If you use many different colors to build the layers, they will be revealed when the felt is cut into.

The Safe Carrier by Gunilla Paetau Sjöberg. 220 × 70 × 75 cm (86 × 27$\frac{1}{2}$ × 29$\frac{1}{4}$ in). This piece was felted like a hat with seams. It is supported with a felt-covered iron armature which follows the pea pod from the bow to the stern. In the bottom is a detachable iron support.

Shapes with Foam-Rubber Cores

In the 1980s, I made a felted jacket embellished with a sheep's head on the shoulder. Because I didn't want the jacket to be too heavy to wear comfortably, I used a foam-rubber core for the sheep's head. I carved the lightweight foam into the shape that I wanted and felted over it. The wool shrank around the form into a strong and firm shape.

Gotland wool or a blend of equal parts of Swedish Fin and Rya are good choices for sculpture. In these fleeces, the outercoat hairs hold together well in the first, vulnerable stage of felting.

Felting around foam rubber

1. With a sharp knife, carve a piece of foam rubber to the desired size and shape. Use a felt-tip pen to draw the shape on the side, top, and front of the foam rubber. Use a knife to carve out the crude shape.

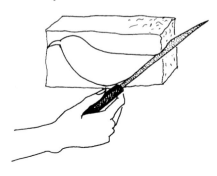

2. Use scissors to cut the final, more precise shape.

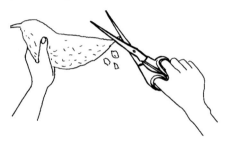

3. For some details, such as the tail and legs of a bird, the foam-rubber shape can be supplemented with plastic-covered wire. Pull a piece of wire through the foam rubber and bend the wire in the middle. Wind strips of carded batt around the wire. These details should be felted first.

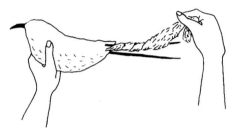

4. Wrap the body with wool batts, crossing them in the same manner that you would for the other techniques. Don't be stingy with the wool: you don't want the foam rubber to show through when the wool begins to shrink. Moisten the wool with a felting solution that has a lot of added soap and carefully massage it. Keep the area where you grip the form damp. Work large shapes on a table and

massage one small area at a time. The wool has a tendency to hang loosely around the form when it is wet, and it is easier to handle when it is resting on a table.

If the resulting form is too indistinct, sharpen it by sewing small stitches with matching thread. Sew through the foam rubber from side to side and pull the stitches together to create details. Roughen up the wool around the stitches with a needle, cover the stitches with this wool, and felt it.

5. Pieces of plastic-covered wire can be used inside the wool of the bird's wings to strengthen and steady them. Full the wings in one direction only.

Bird felted over foam rubber and plastic-coated wire. Maj-Britt Lundaahl.

Hollow Shapes

To make a hollow shape, such as a hat, you will need a template. If you want to felt an irregular shape, first make a small scale model in clay. Then study the proportions and take the necessary measurements. Measure the circumference of all the areas where the dimensions vary. Multiply these measurements to full-scale, add shrinkage allowance as determined by your felt sample, and draw the template. Small details can be formed later by hand.

Cut a template out of strong vinyl and make a sculpture following the instructions for a hat on pages 102–103. Choose a stiff wool such as Rya or Spelsau. If you desire a less hairy surface, use a mixture of equal parts of Rya and fine wool. Coarse Gotland wool will also make a stiff object. Use thick layers to help the form hold its shape. It is best to full around a three-dimensional form, although this may prove cumbersome if you have to hold the support with one hand and full with the other. To help shrink the wool in certain places, use a wooden felting tool (see page 59). After washing and spinning out the water, let the sculpture dry in the desired shape, stuffed with newspaper or suspended.

Stuffing

For added strength, the sculpture can be stuffed and then sewn together in an area where the seam won't show. The best material I've found for stuffing large objects is pieces of foam rubber, which can be purchased from shops that make pillows. Foam rubber is very pliable and can be pushed into any shape.

Wool is too heavy to use as stuffing in large sculptures; however, small items can be stuffed with wool from meat breeds, which has good elasticity and is not suitable for felting.

Polyester stuffing is another, but more expensive, alternative. However, because it is very soft, it does not support large forms well.

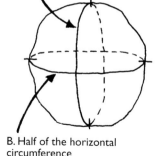

Finished sculpture

A. Half of the vertical circumference

B. Half of the horizontal circumference

Template for a hollow form. Measure the vertical and horizontal circumferences and divide these measurements in half. You

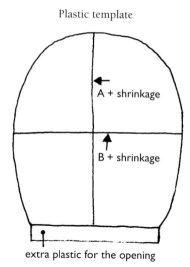

Plastic template

A + shrinkage

B + shrinkage

extra plastic for the opening

must subsequently add the depth and the shrinkage when you make the flat template.

Altar by Gunilla Paetau Sjöberg. Diameter 75 cm (29¹/₄ in), height 65 cm (25¹/₂ in). Felted as a hollow form.

Stiffening

Forms made of thin felt may need additional stiffening to hold their shapes. (See After-Treatments on page 79.) Thick felt of coarse wool will hold its shape without stiffening.

Armatures

Large shapes may require armatures. Chicken wire is a good choice because it can be shaped in many ways. Armature rings and other shapes can be created out of stainless-steel or iron wire rod, which is available in different diameters. Iron should be wrapped with electric tape to keep rust from staining the felt. For very large sculptures, I recommend commissioning an armature skeleton from a blacksmith or welder. Consider making large sculptures in sections that can be assembled and disassembled with bolts or screws so that they can be transported and installed easily.

Foam Rubber Relief Sculpture

Surfaces with relief can be made from solid, compact wool. However, large pieces made this way will be very heavy. Foam rubber cut to shape makes a good base for relief sculpture.

Mankind by Gunilla Paetau Sjöberg. Relief sculpture, detail.

1. Using scissors, cut the desired shape, for example a face, out of foam rubber.

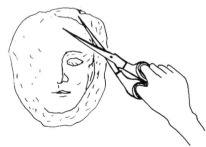

2. Take a piece of unfulled felt and lay it over the foam rubber.

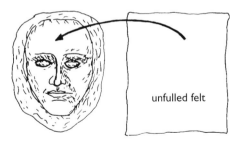

unfulled felt

3. With the felt lying loosely on the foam rubber, use small, straight stitches through the felt and foam rubber to make the desired shape rise out of the felt. For example, define eyebrows and a nose by sewing stitches from side to side, keeping the needle on the right side. Scratch up the wool around the stitches and cover them with it.

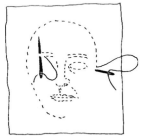

4. Apply felting solution and begin felting. Use a pencil or other fine-tipped tool to work the felt into depressions.

An alternative to foam rubber is polyester batting and quilting. Spread a piece of cloth on a worktable. Lay the batting on top of the cloth and cut into it, layer

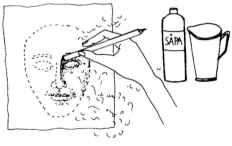

by layer, to get the desired shape. A nose requires many layers! Lay the felt loosely over the batting and pin and tack the layers together. Sew small, straight stitches along all of the important lines, and pull the stitches until the relief is apparent. Apply felting solution and felt until the stitches disappear and the relief form is defined.

If you want an area with very high relief, you can facilitate its formation by stretching that area during felting. Push the shape out from the back side with your finger or an object shaped like the relief you want, and felt from the front with your other hand.

Relief Sculpture by Using Projecting Edges

Wool that can bear its own weight without collapsing, such as Rya and Spelsau, can be used for sculptures with projecting edges that are both durable and well defined. A plastic strip, shaped like the desired projecting edge, is used to shield the projection from the underlying felt during the working stages.

Build the shape from the bottom up. Lay out the wool for the underlayers of the shape and felt up to the point where the projecting edge will be added. Cut out a plastic strip in the shape of the projecting edge. Lay out the wool for the edge over the plastic. Felt the edge so that it attaches to the underlayer of felt along the back side. The edge is easy to shape and harden with a felting tool. Continue building the form upward with more wool.

Fruit and *Virgin of Fire and Void* by Gunilla Paetau Sjöberg. Example of relief with protruding edges.

1. The line where the felt edge will be attached to the underlayer.
2. The line which the projecting edge will follow.

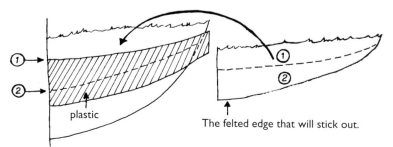

plastic

The felted edge that will stick out.

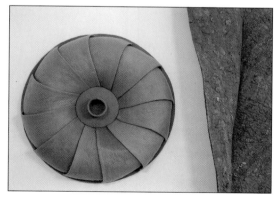

Power by Gunilla Paetau Sjöberg. Detail. Corset ribs are laid between doubled, lightly felted felt and then fulled into the felt to hold out the turbine's blades.

Creating Relief with Appliqué

It is easy to create three-dimensional works with pieces of felt sewn on like appliqué. Felt doesn't fray and can be stretched in all directions.

Pasque Flowers. Felt pieces are appliquéd. The flower centers are small felt balls. The stalks and grass are embroidered with handspun yarn. The felt has been brushed to create a hairy appearance.

Mounting Wall Hangings

Sewing a full lining to felt wall hangings helps preserve the shape of the felt. Wash the lining first to shrink it. Fold under the hem and invisibly whip-stitch the lining to the inside back edge of the felt. You should not be able to see the stitches from the right side. Use an open herringbone stitch a little below the top edge so that the felt will hold its shape when it hangs from attached rings. Sew through the lining into the felt, but not through it. Herringbone stitch can also be sewn just above the bottom edge of the lining to prevent it from hanging below the felt.

Mounting with Velcro

Mounting with Velcro distributes the weight of the felt evenly. The hook side of the tape is sewn to the back of the wall hanging, while the pile side is glued to a wooden slat. The wooden slat can then be attached to the wall.

Mounting with curtain-pleating tape

To mount with curtain-pleating tape, sew the tape to the felt with an overcast stitch. The hooks that fit into the tape should be trimmed with clippers (see illustration) so that the wall hanging can hang flat against the wall, supported by the V-shaped center part of the metal brace.

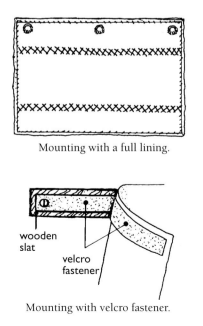

Mounting with a full lining.

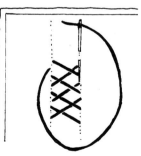

Herringbone stitch.

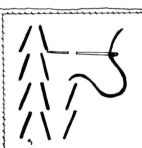

Use tailor's slip stitch to secure the lining in place.

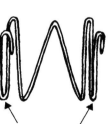

The protruding ends of the hooks are trimmed with clippers.

wooden slat
velcro fastener

Mounting with velcro fastener.

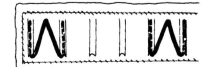

Mounting with curtain-pleating tape.

lining

Whip stitch.

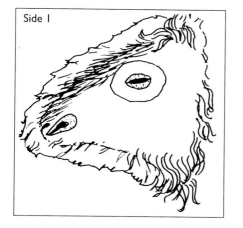

Side 1

Side 2

Masks

A mask can be made in many ways, depending on its character. Avoid using pure Swedish Fin wool for your first mask, as it is the most difficult to shape. Gotland or a blend of equal parts of Rya and Swedish Fin wool are better choices.

Mask in Profile

1. The layout. If the mask is to have a three-dimensional profile, draw it from the side. Cut a template (including a shrinkage allowance) out of thick plastic. Felt it as you would a hat with a front and back side (see pages 102–103).

First, lay out both sides of the mask, face up, with the details placed in mirror image, as shown above. Lay out a fringe of wool for the felt seam on side 1, but don't do so for side 2. Lay the sections on a sheet of cardboard, acrylic, or other plastic.

2. Lay another sheet of plastic on side 1. Using the plastic sheet as a support, turn over the wool so that the inside faces you. Leaving the plastic sheet under the wool so that the details are not displaced, felt it as you would a hat with the opening along the back of the mask's head. Fold the felt seam up around the template.

Baa! by Gunilla Paetau Sjöberg. Mask made in profile.

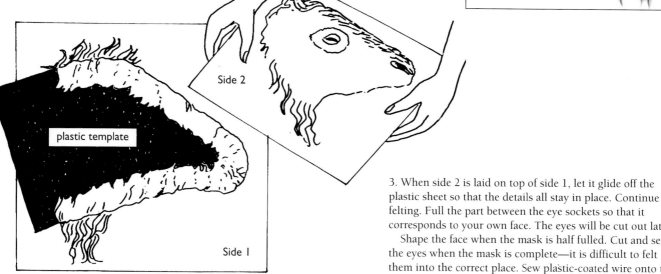

plastic template

Side 2

Side 1

3. When side 2 is laid on top of side 1, let it glide off the plastic sheet so that the details all stay in place. Continue felting. Full the part between the eye sockets so that it corresponds to your own face. The eyes will be cut out later.

Shape the face when the mask is half fulled. Cut and sew in the eyes when the mask is complete—it is difficult to felt them into the correct place. Sew plastic-coated wire onto the outer edge of the mask so that it holds its form.

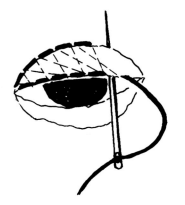

Strengthen the lips, eyes, eyebrows, nose, and other features as needed by using straight and herringbone stitches. Roughen up the wool over the stitches and felt over them to hide them. Cut holes for the eyes and mouth.

Front-Facing Mask
Joszef from Hungary shows his work.

A flat mask can be worked from the front. Lay out the wool to a face shape and size that includes shrinkage and work the wool until it is half fulled. Put your right hand under the felt and push out the nose, forehead, and cheeks. Use different pens or felting tools to press the form in or out as needed.

Elves live in the ceiling in and around a flat row house in Täby, Sweden. They know Marianne Davidson Ekert, feltmaker, who reports:

On a dark November evening, high up in the piles of skins and felt pieces that I save for possible future use, sat an elf who snorted, "At last!"

The elf was precisely as I would have him. He is firm and easy to handle, has a weight in good proportion to his volume, and a face with pronounced features. And he can stand without support!

He has a framework of blasting wire, which is strong and flexible, around which strips of skin are tightly wrapped. Over this is a layer of carded batt to enhance and soften the body shape. The pants are of wool cloth, the jacket of sheepskin, and the hair of naturally dyed yarn. The face and hands are sewn from flesh-colored tricot and bound to the framework. The features are sewn with thread. The hat and shoes are felted in coarsely carded Gotland wool. When the elf was fully clothed and finished, I poured plaster into his boots, put his feet in the boots, and adjusted him so that he stood steady while the plaster set. The elf was totally handmade, inside and out, using several different techniques.

Begin to See and Create

We all carry images in our minds. Some are of things we have seen; others are of abstract experiences. Giving voice to these images can be challenging: it is not always easy to find the right shape, material, or technique to give expression to our feelings.

It is easier to express what we see than what we feel. Depicting nature through art is a good exercise. Translating natural things into other materials gives them a new dimension. Art is your own interpretation of what you see.

Through artistic expression, you can shift reality. You can eliminate, magnify, or distort details to produce something that resembles the object you saw but that has an emotional content that comes from you alone. There are no shortcuts to personal creativity. You can be inspired and learn from other artists, but you must rely on your own vision and voice.

Many textile works are inspired by the color, structure, and texture of the materials themselves. So why not begin there? Experiment freely, without an end result in mind.

After you are familiar with and inspired by the qualities of felt, you will be better equipped to face the larger challenge of making your technical discoveries the means to an end. Set yourself a task. The constraints of that task may result in new techniques you would not have otherwise discovered.

Through your own trials, mistakes, and discoveries, you will learn to evaluate your work and develop your own techniques. These will become your voice, your personal vocabulary. Good luck with your discoveries!

Felt as Art

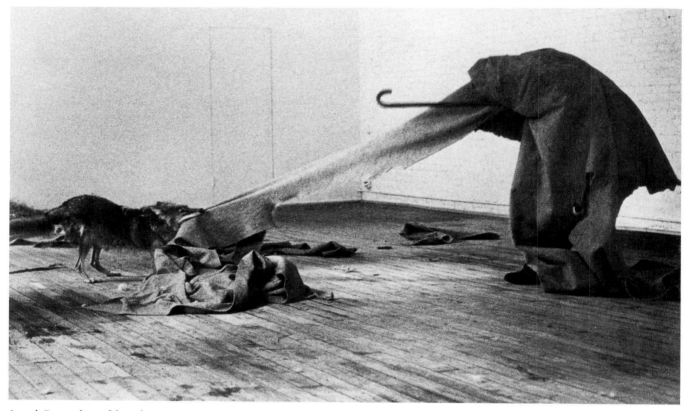

Joseph Beuys shares felt with a coyote in a gallery in New York.

Photograph by Caroline Tisdall, Schirmer/Mosel, Munich.

German artist **Joseph Beuys** (1921–1986) was called "the shaman from Düsseldorf" and was a legend in his own time. The felt hat he perpetually wore was his trademark; he said that it kept his head at an even temperature. He was known for his provoking performances and installations, and for his political ideas, which he shared with his pupils at the art academy in Düsseldorf. The most memorable thing about Beuys is the stubbornness and consistency with which he expressed his ideas on the innermost essence of humankind in relation to modern science and technology.

During World War II, his combat plane was shot down in the Crimea, and he was rescued by nomadic Tatars. They smeared his burned body with lard, wrapped him in felt, and nursed him to health. This incident affected him for the rest of his life. Upon his return to Europe, he interrupted his industrially centered natural science studies and devoted himself to art. His sculptures and drawings often contained symbolic animal motifs; the hare, for example, represented reincarnation and fertility and was also a messenger. Images of the cross, the Earth, and women also appeared in his work. He taught sculpture in Düsseldorf from 1961 to 1972 but was dismissed from the post because of his controversial undertakings. Among other things, he started a student party that called for an autonomous academy and direct democracy. The platform was the "common people's" creative force, total disarmament, and the dissolution of the concept of East and West. The party was large, but "socially acceptable" members were few.

Beuys was not adverse to technology; he strove to bridge the gap between the human spirit and the scientific world. He did live performances full of rites, magic, and incantations. He tried to evoke memories in his audience of a time when people were aligned with nature and the cosmos. His experience with the Tatars awakened his interest in Siberian shamanistic culture—he understood what was necessary to survive and the relationship between warm and cold. Lard and felt were important components of his happenings and installations. The two materials were rolled into pillars, formed a corner of a room, piled into a massive block, functioned as a heating pad, engulfed a grand piano. The hare, dead in his arms, completed the scene.

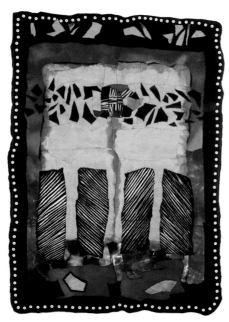

Afton Return, Road Rug Series 3
by **Chad Alice Hagen** 91 x 132 cm (35 x 51 in)

Chad Alice Hagen of St. Paul, Minnesota, works with a variation of mosaic patch-work. Patiently she sews, piece by piece.

The edge of this work is bordered with buttons. The wool is carded Merino, and is dyed with different resist techniques such as tie-dye using acid/metal-complex dyes.

To get a smooth surface on the felt, Chad felts with the rolling technique using a bamboo mat. She works small pieces, about 30 by 30 cm (12 by 12 in), then dyes the felt in several steps until she has achieved the desired color and pattern. She cuts out the shapes and sews them together very tightly.

In previous work, Chad sewed pictures out of partially felted wool and laid motifs down against the bamboo mat. On top of that, she laid five thin layers of dyed wool and then felted it all at the same time. Working on large pieces put a strain on her hands and back, and this led her to her new method. By sewing together fulled felts, she can create large pictures from small modules.

Chad shaves the surface of the felt to remove dirt, pills, grass, and other unwant-ed particles. Shaving also makes the contours of the patterns more distinct. The *Road Rug* series comprises five works that are small enough to fit into a suitcase. By rolling up the felt carpets and taking them along, travelers can create a sense of home, even in a strange environment.

Ovis
by **Beathe-sophie**

Bessie Dammert-Wilcke, who signs her art, Beathe-sophie, lives in Umeå, Sweden. She is inspired by things around her, such as the laboratory chair that she transformed into the sculpture at right.

"I have no special method," she says, "but I work from the idea that different assumptions apply to different circumstances. Characteristic to my work is the way I process the wool to give it a firm and hard surface while retaining its warm and soft nature, especially when it is combined with steel and stone. I use the gray scale in my work to emphasize light, or you could say, I try to emphasize and bring about its excitement and drama."

World Concept
Magic drums inspired **Mari Nagy** and **István Vidák**

During the mid-1980s, the Toy Museum in Kecskemét, Hungary, where Mari Nagy and István Vidák work, was a meeting place for feltmakers from around the world. During the warm weeks of summer, visitors started at the museum and then proceeded out onto the Hungarian *pusta* (prairie) to work together and to swap knowledge and ideas. Many shared felting techniques learned from trips to other lands. Courses and workshops are now offered year round.

Mari and István are driven by a deep interest in the social role of handwork. They are responsible for strong ties between many felters. Their workshops include laughter, play, dance, and music. Their ideal of an ecologically directed community with delight and communication in work, of an animated culture where all people are encouraged to be creative, is realized in their felt work.

Mari and István teach and create their own work. Both are inspired by the early Central Asian relatives of the Hungarians. Shaman drums sing forth from their carpets. They focus on functional art, which they learned from nomads who visited the summer "felt camp". Carpet motifs are cut out of felt and then felted in or formed from carded wool. They use natural dyes.

Surrounding yellow

by **Beret Aksnes.** 285 x 100 x 40 cm (111 x 39 x 16 in)

Beret Aksnes of Trondheim, Norway, began her textile arts career by printing and painting on cloth and machine quilting. Since about 1985, she has dedicated herself to felt. She works with large surfaces that border between two- and three-dimensional expression and experiments with different dyeing techniques.

Beret's special innovation with felt is pleating. We know this technique from Nordic folk dress skirts; it's sometimes called goffering. For her pleating work, Beret uses a thin, even felt, which she has dyed a single background color and will eventually dye with several other colors. After the felt is pleated, it is wrapped tightly with rope and dyed again. For this type of resist dyeing, she uses permanent wool dyes. In most cases, Beret overdyes with black. With the help of an armature constructed of wood and metal, the felt pieces have a third dimension when they are hung.

Beret has also made thrilling clothing of pleated felt.

Corona

by **Maisa Tikkanen.** Diameter 255 cm (99 in)

Maisa Tikkanen has felted many colorful, shimmering coronas. She first experimented with felt in 1972. She got the idea from a film about yurt felting in Turkmenistan. She was captivated by the simplicity of the technique; no special tools were needed. Maisa lives in Punkaharju, Finland, surrounded by nature, which is the basis for her art.

Maisa lays out thin layer upon layer of many different colors so that the surface shimmers with color. The directional placement of the long fibers creates stripes in her compositions that most often radiate from the center. The work is only lightly fulled so that all of the color transitions and fiber directions are distinguishable. Careful mounting makes the work durable. She buys wool already dyed and carded.

Maisa has built a studio for feltwork in an old barn on a farm in Kulennoinen. Before she had the studio, she worked on large projects outside in the yard and in the sauna. The Finnish sauna, with its hot, moist air, is the perfect environment for manufacturing felt.

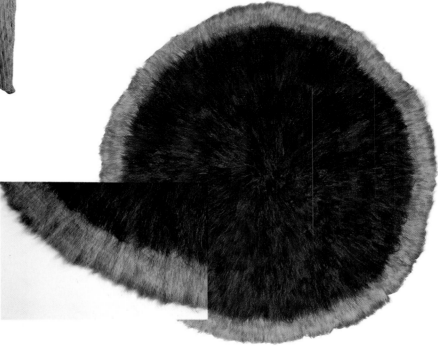

Felt Home

Tuula, from Angelniemi, Finland, is known for her brightly colored, fantasy clothing. Actually, it is more than clothing. She creates magical, ritualistic costumes full of stories and meanings. They are based in anthropology and theater.

Tuula abandoned the creation of clothing for another form of felt covering, the tent. She began with a gaudy tent framework,

by **Tuula Isojunno-Nikulainen**.

Homage to the Nomads. This construction, which has wood felted into it, was shown at the Lausanne Biennale in 1992. Her next creation was a covered *ger* called *Felt Home.* The tent combines the ancient and the modern, as does her clothing. When working, Tuula weighs nothing, measures nothing; she works intuitively, from her soul.

Etamin

Silja Puranen lives in Järvenpää, Finland. The theme in her work since 1991 is time: the relationship between humankind and time, between a second and eternity. Silja combines wool with other materials during the felting process. The outermost layer is flax to give the work more life, lightness, and sheen, and a more expressive character. She often uses hard, stick-like fibers to complete or continue a shape or to create contrast.

In *Etamin*, Silja used wool, flax, coconut fiber, and bassine (a fiber which is similar to but somewhat thinner, softer, and weaker than palm fiber.)

Silja usually purchases wool in different colors and cards them together to produce

by **Silja Puranen**. 55 x 260 cm (22 x 102 in)

the desired color. She dyes the flax herself with fiber-reactive dyes. The flax is laid on top and felted into the wool. The wool fiber shrinks over the flax, and the flax has the ability to felt on its own, like cellulose fiber in paper.

The sticks in the work are hard vegetable fibers such as coconut fiber, bassine, and palm. Silja uses coconut fiber on the surface. The fibers are attached when the wool and flax are felted. When she uses a large quantity of coconut fiber on the surface, she lays a thin layer of flax on top of it.

Palm and bassine are used on the edge. These fibers lie between layers of wool, so that they lodge into the felt.

Felt Projects

Clothing

Using the Asiatic rolling technique, jacket fabric can be made from carded batts in just a few hours.

Man's jacket of Swedish Fin wool by Gunilla Paetau Sjöberg. The felt was fulled in the washing machine. The edge is bound with a knitted band, and the buttonholes are machine sewn.

Choosing Wool Types

The garment you intend to make should dictate the type of wool to choose. A garment that is to be worn against the skin requires soft, fine wool. Lamb's wool is a possibility, though it is a bit nubby. A jacket that will be exposed to rain and wind should be rugged and needs a wool such as Gotland wool. Choose a wool with enough undercoat to

hold the slippery overcoat in the felt. Leicester yields a pretty cloth with a fine sheen. Even Rya lamb's wool can be used for clothing fabric—and the outercoat fiber is water resistant. Use it as the outer layer of a garment with fine wool on the inside. The coarser types of wools can be felted together with a layer of fine wool to make the felt soft and flexible.

Advantages and disadvantages of wool types are discussed on pages 37–38.

Carding and Blending Fibers

Read the section on carding (page 47) before you begin carding the wool. When making clothing, you must be certain of your materials. Because felt is easily abraded, it is best to use the premium parts of a fleece. A large jacket will probably require two fleeces, which should have similar qualities. Use the best staple from the back and sides and remove any second cuts. For a smooth cloth, the wool must be carded at least twice. If you use a drum carder, card curly wool three times. Hold each carded batt up to the light to ensure that there are no thick or thin areas: the carded wool must be uniform if the felt is to shrink and absorb dye evenly. After the first carding, blend wool from different fleeces or different parts of the same fleece.

Commercially Carded Batts versus Home Carding

Very thin felt requires thin, even batts. Either hand carders or a carding bench will work for small projects; however, both require a lot of effort to process the large quantity of wool necessary to make a large piece such as a garment or wall hanging.

It is more difficult to make thin and even batts with a drum carder. You must card the first batt as thinly and evenly as possible, then remove it from the carder and weigh it. Then you must weigh out piles fleece of exactly the same weight and run them through the drum carder exactly the same way to achieve the same batt quality.

Commercially carded batts are large and uniform in thickness. They can be separated as thinly as desired. You may find it helpful to purchase fine wool as commercially carded batts, because it is the most difficult to card uniformly.

Designs and Patterns

Even by itself, handmade felt is beautiful. So why not use a simple design that will show off the material? Remember that felt has a certain rigidity which should be allowed to come forth; it is sculptural and does not drape as softly as woven fabric.

You can get many styling ideas by playing with a piece of finished felt cloth in front of a mirror. For example, wavy edges can make an attractive peplum or intriguing cuffs.

Sketch your ideas and play upon the

simple suggestions in this book. If you begin with a commercial pattern, simplify it and remove unnecessary details. Felt is more unwieldy than woven cloth—it can be too bulky to gather into a band. Avoid inset collars, loops, and other details that would be difficult to sew in felt. Also, choose a larger size than you would normally use. Felt fabric will require more space for ease of movement.

Before you make felt cloth for a garment, read through the sections on laying out the pattern and sewing that follow, so that you will be sure to have a piece of fabric large enough for the garment you want to make.

If you want to decorate or dye the fabric, read the sections on felting designs (page 68), dyeing (page 44), and printing (page 45).

Dyed wool staples make a design on top of undyed wool. The felt was dyed after it was fulled, overdyeing the wool staples.

Don't Forget the Felt Sample

Making a sample is critical if disappointments are to be avoided.

Follow the instructions for making thin felt with the rolling technique (page 64). Make both a thin and a thick variation. For the thin cloth, make the wool batts so thin that when you lay them out you can see the supporting material through the first layer of wool and a hint of it through the second layer. You will get a denser, more durable cloth by laying out the wool thinly and then shrinking it a lot than by laying it out thickly and only shrinking it a little. The finished sample will indicate

- whether you laid out the wool to the correct thickness. Is the cloth as thin as you would like it?
- whether the fabric is durable. Let the sample dry and then "rub" it. Do the fibers loosen?
- whether the image is what you expected. If the image is indistinct, the motif felt was either too thin or too loosely felted.
- the percent of shrinkage. By measuring the sample before and after felting, you can figure out the percent of shrinkage and then figure out how much wool you will need for the garment. Remember that long-haired wool gives a sense of nap and direction to the cloth and that you may need a larger piece of fabric to allow for this.

Felting

Using the information gained from your sample, felt your cloth. As you felt, continue to pull out any creases, rub the edges tightly, and control the evenness. Lay more wool on areas that seem too thin. Stretch the felt neatly as you roll it up. Near the end of the fulling process, knead the fabric by hand for a little while in a basin until you're satisfied with the feel of the felt (see page 67).

Wash out the felting solution with a mild laundry detergent and rinse several times, adding a little vinegar in the last rinse. Spin out the excess water or hang the cloth until it is half dry; smooth out the felt. While the cloth is still only half dry, run it through a mangle or press it with a hot iron and pressing cloth.

Laying Out the Garment Pattern

Before you lay out a garment pattern, examine the quality of the felt. Look for any thin or thick areas, flaws, or color stains. Mark them with pins or tacking stitches so that you will know where they are and can either correct them or avoid

them when you cut out the pattern pieces.

You also must take into account the nap, if any, in the felt. If your felt has a layer of long-haired wool, place the straight-of-grain arrows printed on the pattern pieces along the grain of the long fiber and turn the felt so that the hair layer will be on the garment's outer face. Not only will this give the garment a uniform look, but the rain will run right off it.

If you use only short, fine wool in your felt, place the pattern pieces parallel to either the width or the length of the fabric, whichever gives the best fit, provided that the design on the cloth allows this.

Lay out the pattern on a single layer of cloth if the felt is thick. Pattern pieces that are to be placed along a fold should be first cut out of paper so that the complete paper pattern can be laid on a single thickness of felt. Not only is a single layer of felt easier to cut out, but full pattern pieces are easier to lay out.

Collars and other details can be quite

Vest in Two Sections. Swedish Fin wool of the Gobelin type with a thin layer of Rya lamb's wool on the surface, by Gunilla Paetau Sjöberg. Decorated with inlaid, dyed wool staples. The felt was dyed after fulling. The size of this style is easy to alter at the seams. For ideas on making designs in felt, see page 68.

simple if the felt is well fulled and not overly thin. You can also felt these details separately, and make them extra thick.

The width of the seam allowance depends on the type of seam you plan to use. Cut the seams neatly so that you won't have to mark the seam lines.

Sewing

Sample to determine which seam treatment and stitch length are appropriate for the thickness of your felt. A stitch length of 2.5 to 3 millimeters (about 1/8 inch) is usually sufficient.

Because it is difficult to sew darts in thick fabrics, shape felt garments by easing in the excess cloth with a doubled gathering thread and pressing it with an iron. Darts may be sewn in thin felt, but only if the garment requires a lot of shaping.

Pin the pieces together at the seams, try on the garment, and adjust the seams as necessary.

Plan the order in which you will sew the seams. For a simple loose-fitting top with flexible sleeves, it is easiest to sew the shoulder seams first, sew the sleeves to the body, and then fold the garment in half and sew the side, underarm, and sleeve seams in one sweep from the lower edge of the

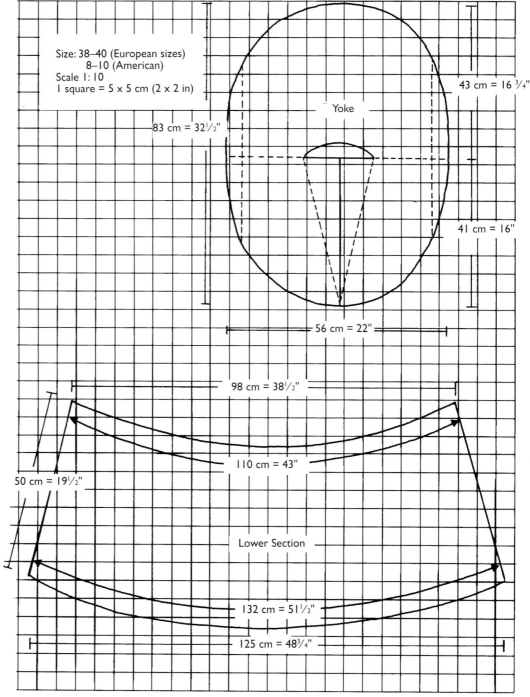

Size: 38–40 (European sizes)
8–10 (American)
Scale 1:10
1 square = 5 x 5 cm (2 x 2 in)

43 cm = 16 ¾"

Yoke

83 cm = 32½"

41 cm = 16"

56 cm = 22"

98 cm = 38½"

110 cm = 43"

50 cm = 19½"

Lower Section

132 cm = 51½"

125 cm = 48¾"

Pattern for the vest in two sections. The yoke is made from an oval that is folded over the shoulders. The opening for the neck and center front is cut after fulling. To determine the placement of the shoulder line and neck opening, fold the oval in half

and measure 2 to 2.5 cm (3/4 to 1 in) forward from the foldline. The front of the yoke should be 2 to 2.5 cm (3/4 to 1 in) shorter than the back so that the vest will not slide backward.

Fold in a facing along the armholes and

neck opening on the dotted lines. The cut edges are fulled with warm water for a more finished look.

Sew the vest together by hand with running stitches. Sew the facings in place.

body to the cuff. For garment designs with rigid sleeves, sew the shoulder seam first, followed by the side seams, then sew the sleeve seams and put the sleeves into the armholes.

Try on the garment in front of a mirror and experiment with different ways to finish the neck. You might want a facing, a collar, or just a cut edge. Remove the garment and mark a neck opening. Put the garment back on and check that the marked opening is correct. Cut one-half of the neck, allowing for the seam allowance, and then mark and cut the other half of the neck opening.

Make a facing for the neck opening out of lining material (most felt is too thick) or sew on a collar. For thin, fine garments of well-fulled felt, the neck opening can be nothing more than a cleanly cut edge that has been finished with light felting (using warm water without felting solution). You can finish other cut edges the same way.

Felt that you suspect might be abraded or that is loosely fulled can benefit from a band-covered edge. Flexible felt can be folded under for hems and button bands. Thick jackets can tolerate thick folds. Sample your felt to discover what will work!

Be particular when choosing notions and accessories. Use knitted all-wool bands, which are flexible and easy to shape along the garment edges or seams. Dye the bands in the dyebath with the felt cloth—you will seldom find just the right color in the store. Avoid purchased ribbing, which rarely has the same character as felt. Make buttons out of felt balls or cover over old buttons with felt.

Garments made of fine wool do not need to be lined. Jackets can be lined with silk. Dye the lining with wool dyes if you want the colors to coordinate. You may want to line outerwear with wind-resistant cotton poplin.

Vest felted in one piece, by Gunilla Paetau Sjöberg. The design was inspired by snow melting in a field. A folded double felt edge is sewn around the neck and front edge. The vest was felted according to the same principle as the hat but with openings for the neck and arms. When laying out the wool, make the neck and arm openings smaller than you want them to be in the finished garment: they will enlarge during felting. To shape a vest like this, cut holes for your arms and neck in a full-sized trash bag, slip it on, slip on the vest, and form the vest on your body in front of a mirror during the last stages of fulling.

Felt jacket and hat with checked design of felted-in inlaid yarn, by Britt Karin Tuflått and Johanne Moe Nyland, Norway.

Dress with a bodice of "wool cloqué" (see page 71) and a skirt of synthetic organza, by Gunilla Paetau Sjöberg.

Naturally dyed, knitted cardigan with yoke of synthetically dyed felt. The yoke is decorated and strengthened with couched handspun yarn. The yoke was made in the same way as the blue vest on page 95, and was sewn to the knitted fabric on its lower edge. The front bands were knitted.

"Anti-depression" jacket made in 1981, by Gunilla Paetau Sjöberg and worn between September and April for ten years! The jacket is made from high-quality Gotland wool and cut from the same pattern used for the blue vest on page 95, allowing for more ease. Stuffing is inserted into folds of felt to stiffen the outer edges of the shoulders. The sleeves are set into the armhole and sewn to the folded flap at the shoulders along with Baartil and Baarta, sheep heads made as described on page 82. The jacket is also embellished with embroidery and appliqué and is closed with hook-and-eye closures.

Felt jacket made from two layers of Gotland wool, by Mia Fallman. The bottom layer was well carded, and the top layer was run through the drum carder only once, giving the felt a strong texture. The fabric was dyed after felting. The jacket was easily sewn because the sleeve pattern is connected to the torso piece. The pillbox hat is made with the same material. The purse is made by felting around a cookie tin (see page 114).

Felt Seams

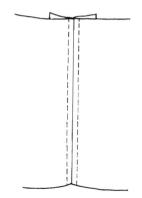

Seam pressed open and top-stitched along the seam allowance.

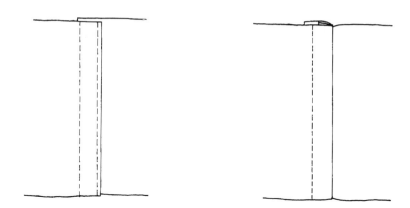

Overlap seam for thick felt. Using tailor's chalk, mark the seam line about 1 cm (3/8 in) in on the bottom piece. Lay the edge of the top piece along the mark, pin, and stitch.

Fell seam with open edge.

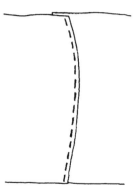

Hand-sewn overlap with running stitch. Use button and carpet thread or buttonhole silk.

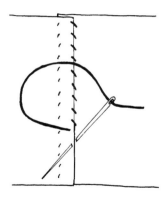

Hand-sewn overlap with hem stitching on each side.

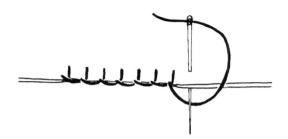

Blanket stitch sewn through two layers makes a tight seam for mittens and slippers.

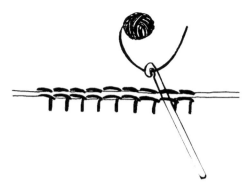

Crocheting together two edges that were first edged with blanket stitch. This technique makes a smooth but noticeable seam. It is used in such items as caps.

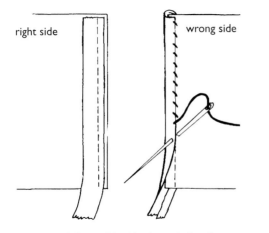

right side   wrong side

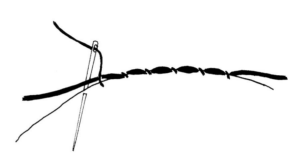

Edging with a thick yarn, such as handspun, or with a cord of wool yarn. The thick yarn is couched down with a thinner yarn. The edge can also be crocheted, knitted, faced with felt, or just clipped cleanly (see pages [149, 150, and 166]).

Edging with knitted band. The wide band is sewn to the garment, right sides together, and then folded over to the back side and overcast in place. Be aware that knitted bands will shrink in length when dyed!

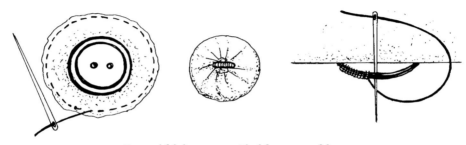

Covered felt buttons are ideal for coarser felt fabrics. Cover a purchased button with felt. Use a loop of button and carpet thread for the buttonhole.

Tailor's marking paper seldom works well on felt. Use tailor's chalk instead. Fine-tipped waterproof felt pens can be used to draw embroidery designs and text onto the felt. Press the point down through the pattern paper so that small dots appear on the felt.

Hats and Caps

Hats and other head coverings can be made in a variety of ways. A fisherman's hat should be thick for warmth and should have a hairy surface so that the rain will run off. On the other hand, an elegant dress hat should be smooth, thin, and hard-felted. Before you begin felting a hat, consider which functions and which qualities you want it to have.

The fulling technique can greatly affect the look of the finished hat. Felting boards of wood are effective, but they tend to pull up the fibers and give the surface of the felt a hairy appearance. Felting boards also produce a nubby surface and a thicker felt. If you want a thinner hat with a smooth surface, use the rolling technique.

Pages 102–103 give instructions for felting a coarse fisherman's hat. It is made in the traditional Swedish rubbing method, unlike the patterned hats shown on page 105, which were made with the rolling technique. Try this technique with medium-coarse wool first, which is easiest to handle.

Happy fishermen protected from the cold and elements by felted hats. Wide brims direct rainwater away from the collar.

Hat in Gotland wool felted with the rubbing technique, by Gunilla Paetau Sjöberg.

Hats are appropriate attire for gentlemen in all lines of business. These were made of Swedish Fin wool of the Gobelin type by Gunilla Paetau Sjöberg.

Coarse Fisherman's Hat Made with the Rubbing Technique

Material

About 130 grams (4½ ounces) Gotland wool, coarser Swedish Fin wool of the Gobelin type, or Leicester. Divide the wool into two equal parts, one for the front side and one for the back. Divide these two wool piles into two parts each, one for each layer.

Pattern

Make a template by drawing a bell-shaped pattern on thick vinyl following the measurement shown below. Fold the vinyl in half before cutting out the template to make sure that the two sides are symmetrical.

Width: measure the head circumference where the hat will sit, divide by 2, and add on the percent of shrinkage which depends on the quality of the wool.

Example:

Width = circumference 58 cm ÷ 2 = 29 cm + shrinkage (40%) 11.6 cm = 40.6 cm.

Height = crown height + brim width + percent of shrinkage.

Example: Height = brim 13 cm + crown 17 cm = 30 cm + shrinkage (40%) 12 cm = 42 cm.

Width = circumference 23 in ÷ 2 = 11 1/2 in + shrinkage (40%) 4½ in = 16 in.

Height = crown height + brim width + percent of shrinkage.

Height = brim 5 in + crown 6¾ in = 11¾ in + shrinkage (40%) 4¾ in = 16½ in.

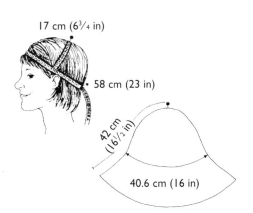

Calculation of hat template.

Felting

1. Lay out two crisscrossing layers of carded wool according to the template, allowing for a seam allowance of about 3 cm (1¼ in) around the crown. Pull on the seam allowance to thin it out. Note: there is no seam allowance along the lower edge of the brim.

2. Pour felting solution over the back of your hand so that the water is spread out over the wool. Note: do not put water on the seam allowance or it will be difficult to fold it over the template without creating a flap during felting. Put the

template on the wool and press down on it so that all the air is pushed out and the water extends to the template's edge.

3. Pour a little felting solution on top of the template for lubrication and with the palms of your hands gently massage the template into the wool. Remove the template after a few minutes and work directly on the wool with circular movements. Concentrate your work in the middle of the hat. When the fibers are lightly felted, lay the template back on the wet wool and fold the seam allowance up over the plastic. Moisten the

seam allowance lightly and press it down. Take care to fold the wool exactly at the edge of the template to prevent wool from felting together along the edge, which will create a flap.

4. Add the wool for the other side, pulling out the fibers in the seam allowance to thin it. Lay the wool in the same direction as the previous layer, but lay the following layer in the opposite direction. It is important for the long fiber to have the same orientation in the outermost layers of both sides of the hat for the finished felt to look its best.

5. Pour on felting solution, press down the wool, and carefully massage the entire surface except for the seam allowance. After a while, place your hand inside the hat on top of the plastic and rub together the top layer and the seam allowance from the bottom layer.

6. When the top layer of wool has been felted, carefully turn over the hat. Then fold the seam allowance over to this side and massage the hat along the outer and inner edge to help it attach.

Felt the entire back side. Place your hand inside the hat and rub around the fold to prevent a felted ridge or flap from forming there. If one does form, try to pull out the flap with mild pressure by taking hold of the felt on either side of the flap and pulling. If the felting process has progressed too far, you can either be satisfied with a hat that has a flap running across the crown, or be brave and carefully cut the fiber from the inside the hat in the middle of the flap. Be careful not to cut too deeply. After cutting, carefully rub apart the cut area. (Making this cut is not recommended, but what can you do in the face of disaster? You'll make this mistake just once. . . .)

7. Now work a little bit with the edge of the brim. The edge is most commonly cut after it has been fulled, but with a little practice you can learn to felt it to the correct breadth and evenness. Work the brim in circles with your hand over the edge, moving from the outside in toward the crown. This motion makes the edge tighter and causes fibers that stick out to work themselves into the felt. Do not fold in any fibers along the edge; felt them in instead. Stretch out the brim after the wool becomes felt. Felt and stretch in turns until you are satisfied with the shape of the brim.

8. When the felting stage is complete, all seam allowances and folds are controlled, and the brim edge has been felted and shaped, it is time for fulling. Lay a piece of cloth under the hat to protect the wool. (The template can still be inside the hat—when the wool has shrunk so that the template is now too big, it will come out by itself.) Roll up the cloth and hat together, first from the sides (vertically) to bring in the width of the crown. Rub the roll against the felting board, so that the felt works itself into the cloth. Roll the hat from another direction and rub against the felting board again. Refold the hat so that the foldline is in a different place. Be careful not to shrink the hat too much—it will shrink more in the width when it is washed and dyed.

9. Roll the hat down from the top (horizontally). After working this direction for a while, reroll it down from the brim. After a while, make the fold in a different part of the hat, and roll it until all of the fabric shrinks back. Using a bamboo mat instead of a felting board produces a smooth surface.

10. Tug the hat onto a hat block. (If the hat is still much too big, continue to rub it on the felting board.) Press the crown down onto the hat block and work the top with your hands or with a wooden felting tool. Work around the entire crown. Decide where you want the crown line, wrap a string twice around this line, pull it tight, and knot it; or position a strong, large rubber band along the crown line. This cord or band will stay on the block as you work.

11. Full the brim to the desired width and stiffness. This goes quickly with the felting tool and will save wear and tear on your hands. While fulling the brim, you can set the hat on a table. Then put the hat back on the hat block and shape the whole form. Work the border between the brim and crown with a felting tool to clearly delineate the crown line.

12. Wash the hat, dye it if desired, and then rinse it, spin the water out, and shape it again on the hat block. Let the hat dry in the desired shape on newspaper.

13. When the hat is nearly dry, press the crown on the hat block and the brim on an ironing board using a damp pressing cloth and a hot iron. The pressing and subsequent cooling help to set the shape. Several pressings will stabilize the form.

A fisherman's hat should be slightly floppy and should require no additional dressing or stiffening. But if you want to apply a finish to the hat, see the section on after-treatments (page 79).

Most beginner hat projects are gray, perhaps because Gotland wool is so easy to work with. Students at the Väddö Folk High School model their first feltmaking projects. (*Translator's note: A Swedish folk high school is a cross between the senior year of an American high school and the freshman year at a community college. Students complete their regular schooling at age sixteen.*)

With decorations and brim shapings, every hat gets its own style. Jennie Arvidsson, Carina Grönlund, and Maria Bohlin at the Väddö Folk High School.

Grass hat, by Lena Kilpelä, Finland. Lena uses Finnish Landrace wool. Many of her hats have an interesting detail in the middle of the crown.

Jorie Johnson's hats

Jorie Johnson is an American who studied textile design at the Rhode Island School of Design and later in Finland. She now lives in Japan, where she makes felt clothing, hats, accessories, tea carpets for tatami mats, and experimental artworks. She also teaches feltmaking.

One of Jorie's specialties is hats with inlaid motifs. She fulls exclusively with the rolling technique, which produces a very smooth surface. A unique part of her technique is that the design is laid down on the template, and then the background or base fiber is put on top of it. This makes the design attach well. The wool is then felted and fulled.

Here is how she does it.

1. Weigh out 60 to 90 grams (2 to 3 ounces) of wool. Jorie prefers coarse Merino or New Zealand halfbred 58s and also blends Corriedale with coarse Merino. The amount of wool needed will depend on the size of the hat brim. Card the wool and divide it into two equal parts, one for each side of the hat.

2. Draw a bell shape on a piece of cardboard 3 millimeters (1/8 inch) thick. Cardboard is ideal for the template because it is easy to feel the edge underneath the layers of wet wool. The width of the bell should be half of the head circumference plus shrinkage allowance (about 40 to 45 percent); the height should be the desired hat height plus the width of the brim plus shrinkage. Cut the shape out to make a template.

3. Make a design of cut, lightly felted pieces of motif felt, silk organza, and yarn that is at least 70 percent wool, mohair, or other animal fiber. Prepare enough for both sides of the hat.

4. Lay out the design motif on the cardboard template, right side down. Sprinkle a bit of felting solution on top of the design to make it cling to the cardboard. Press a piece of thin plastic that is larger than the template on top of the

design and turn everything over so that the plastic is on the bottom and the template is on top.

5. Arrange the design for the other side of the hat on the template, right side down. Fold any elements from the underside that extend beyond the edge of the template over the edge to the top side. Cover the design with background wool (one half of the weighed-out carded batts). Lay out at least two layers of batts

at right angles to one another. The batts should extend just to the edge of the template; when the wool is wet, it will extend just beyond the edge, making a seam allowance.

6. Place a fine, stiff nylon net, such as mosquito netting, on top of the laid-out batts. Sprinkle the net with felting solution and press down on it with your hands to push the air out and thoroughly wet the wool.

7. Replace the net with a sheet of plastic and turn the packet over. Remove the plastic from what is now the upper side. Gently pull out the seam allowances and fold them over right against the edge of the template. Avoid creating any wrinkles or heavily gathered areas, especially at the corners.

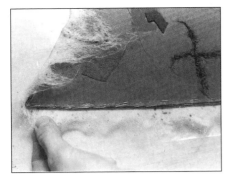

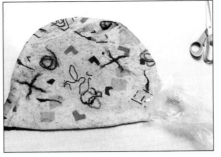

8. Position the other half of the weighed-out wool on top of the design, then repeat steps 6 and 7. If it is difficult to keep the edges in place, sprinkle them with more solution until the wool relaxes.

Note: In addition to exciting inlaid designs, most of Jorie's hats have a different color for the inside and outside. This is accomplished by choosing two base colors, dividing them into four equal weights, and performing steps 5 through 8 twice. This simple technique allows for interesting color combinations without too much additional effort.

9. With your hands in thin plastic sandwich bags or gloves, begin felting by carefully caressing the wool, starting from the outer edges and working toward the middle.

10. Gently massage the surface, gradually increasing finger pressure as the wool begins to tighten. When the fabric is firm and the inner design begins to appear through the base, pinch and pull the surface to see if the fabric is strong enough to cut for removal of the template. When the felt is firm, use sharp scissors to cut the lower edge of the bell 0.6 cm (1/4 in) from the bottom. Save

the narrow scrap for use as a decorative trimming later.

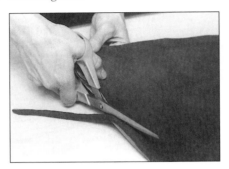

11. Open out the lower edge of the hat and massage from the inside. Make sure that the design has attached to the base and remove the template. Turn the hat right side out and adjust or add to the design if desired. Continue working the design into the base, adding extra solution if necessary. You can also apply bar soap directly onto the surface; this creates a small number of bubbles which help ease the design into the base. When you are confident that the design has felt-

ed into the background, turn the hat inside out again and place some plastic inside to separate the two sides of the hat.

12. Lay out a sheet of plastic that is slightly larger than the hat on a sturdy table and place the hat on top of it. Begin fulling by rolling the hat and plastic around a rod that is 3.8 centimeters (1½ inches) in diameter and a bit longer than the width of the bell of the hat. Tightly roll this bundle into a cotton cloth or

towel; this will absorb excess wetness and aid in keeping everything neatly rolled. Standing with your feet spread slightly apart, begin rolling with outstretched arms from the tips of your fingers to your elbows, applying your upper body weight. It is not muscle exertion that is required here but rather comfortable and rhythmic rolling. Roll back and forth a few times and then roll the hat up in another direction. Carefully stretch out the brim, roll the felt in another direction, stretch the brim, roll, stretch.

13. As the hat shrinks and stiffens, begin working on the brim. Moisten the brim with felting solution and roll up a portion of it on a smooth dowel about 1.5 by 20 centimeters (1/2 by 8 inches); roll toward the inside of the hat forty times. Roll the next portion in the same manner. Continue working around the

edge until the entire brim has been rolled. Flip the hat inside out and repeat the process. If you want a really stiff brim, you may have to repeat the process a third or fourth time. Although you are working only on the brim, be aware that the rest of the hat will shrink as well from the agitation.

14. When the brim is adequately rolled, it is time to work on the crown. Place the hat on a form such as a wooden hat block, bowl, ball, or other object. (You can easily make a fine hat block by carving the shape out of dense Styrofoam and covering it with a thin plastic bag and a nylon stocking.) Wrap a piece of elastic 4 centimeters (1½ inches) wide around the juncture of the crown and brim. This keeps the hat in position while you pull the crown into shape.

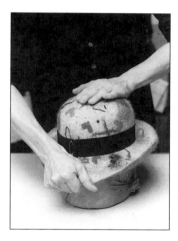

15. When you are satisfied with the stiffness, size, and shape, rinse the hat and spin out the excess water. Stretch the hat back onto the block and replace the elastic around the base of the crown. For a slight variation in form, pinch up about 3 centimeters (1⅛ inches) at the center of the crown. Pinch up a crease from this point down the side of the crown; this line should taper off and end at the crown line. Pin in place. Once the crease has set, smooth the brim and press the entire hat with a hot steam iron. Let the hat air dry. Trim any fuzzy hairs off the brim and embellish your creation with

ribbon, stitching, or other decorative element.

Note: If the hat is going to be dyed, leave it a bit big to allow for shrinkage during dyeing. Fine wool fibers may shrink more than coarse ones in a hot, acid dyebath because the scales will open up and more felting will occur. After dyeing and rinsing, finish the hat as described in step 15.

Beret of Swedish Fin wool by Gunilla Paetau Sjöberg and Mia Fallman. A beret is felted without an opening for the head. The opening is cut when felting is near completion, and the template is removed. This beret is 29 centimeters (11½ inches) in diameter. The template was 44 centimeters (17 inches) in diameter; there was about 45 percent shrinkage, which is appropriate for Swedish Fin wool.

To make a beret, follow the instructions for the first two steps of the cookie-tin purse (page 114), but lay out just two thin layers of carded batts. After felting, full the wool by carefully rolling it. Cut an opening in the middle of the beret's underside. If you desire height in the beret, cut the opening a bit smaller than your head size and stretch it out. After dyeing, edge with grosgrain ribbon or leather.

Hat by Marit Rehn, Stenebyskolan (a well-known Swedish craft school), Dals Långed, Sweden.

Vesla Schau felts hats professionally in Norway. In Norway, wool is sorted and classified at sorting stations, where craftspeople can choose exactly the quality of wool that they want. Vesla sends her chosen fleece to a commercial carder for washing and carding.

For her fine hats, Vesla uses fine-fibered wool with good crimp such as Merino, Finnish Landrace, or Dalasau lamb's wool. This type of fiber gives a tight and soft quality to the felt. On the outer surface of some of her hats, Vesla places a very thin layer of coarser wool to give the hats more sheen. Hats made of coarse wool need a thin layer of finer wool to make the felt tight. Vesla uses large templates, lays out the wool very thinly, and shrinks it as much as 60 to 70 percent to produce a very strong and tight felt. For a hat weighing 100 grams (3 1/2 ounces), Vesla uses two thin batts of 50 grams (1 3/4 ounces) each, carefully controlling the evenness and direction of the wool as she lays it out. She uses a seam allowance of about 3 centimeters (1 1/4 inches). When she uses very fine wool, Vesla lays out just one layer of carded batts on each side, aligning the fibers vertically in the hat. She explains that a single layer of fine wool is adequate if care is taken to make the layer even when laying out the wool and felting it. She begins by fulling the hat only in the vertical direction (brim to crown) to shrink the fibers together. Vesla finds that having just one layer of wool in this alignment makes the brim easier to stretch out and shape.

Using the rubbing technique, Vesla felts together the edge of the brim and then cuts it open. After the template has been removed, she felts the brim a bit more, rinses the hat carefully, and dyes it with acid dyes. Then she fulls the hat in a bamboo mat by rolling it from side to side to shrink the width. Vesla neatly straightens out the hat between each rolling. Then she rolls the hat in the other direction (from top to bottom), leaving the bottom edge of the brim outside the mat.

To finish shrinking the hat, Vesla puts it into boiling water, presses it over a hat block, and rubs warm felting solution into the crown and brim. After rinsing it well, she immerses it in a vinegar/water solution for about 10 minutes. Then she spins the water out, shapes the hat on a hat block, and presses and steams it with an iron until the felt is smooth and fine.

Vesla finishes her hats with a grosgrain ribbon sweatband. She sews piano wire or hat wire to the outer edge of the brim on some hats and hides the wire with a strip of leather. She uses hat dressing (see the section on after-treatments on page 79) to help hold the shape.

Felt Socks and Boots

Boots inspired by Torgut boots, embellished with embroidery, by Susanne Tholin.

A Torgut woman in Mongolia wearing traditional *toku* boots with rawhide soles and knotted with leather thongs. Her grandchild wears felt boots made in a factory.

Outdoor boot of densely fulled Gotland wool, dyed after fulling, by Gunilla Paetau Sjöberg. The final stage of fulling was done in the washing machine with a hard foam-rubber template inside the boot. The snake was sewn on afterward. Rubber soles can be glued onto boots with contact cement.

Socks

These directions are simplified. If you have not felted before, read the sections on felting with the rubbing technique (page 61) and felting a coarse hat (page 102), which describes three-dimensional felting in detail.

Draw a template by standing on a piece of thick vinyl and drawing around your foot, extending a shaft to one side. Draw another line outside the first to allow for the correct shrinkage (to determine shrinkage, see page 56). Straighten out the inside curve under foot and the heel when drawing the template. The sock will get its shape when it is fulled.

Gotland wool or a mixture of Rya and Swedish Fin wool will make a strong sock if they are fulled hard. Weigh the wool before beginning the first sock and then weigh what is left afterward so that you will know how much wool to use for the second sock.

1. Lay out at least two layers of batts as illustrated. A thick boot will require three to four layers of wool. Lay several extra layers of wool along the sole. Lay out both sides of the sock at the same time as shown, leaving no seam allowance under the sole.

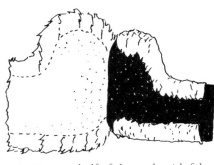

2. Wet one-half of the sock with felting solution. Keeping the seam allowances dry, lightly felt the wool. Repeat for the other half of the sock. Tear the seam allowances apart along the fold line at the sole of the sock. Fold the seam allowances over the template on one side and moisten them lightly so they stay down.

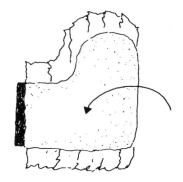

3. Quickly fold this side of the sock over the other, making sure that the fold along the sole is snug against the edge of the template.

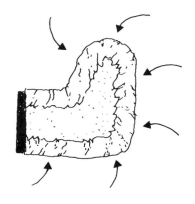

4. Fold over the seam allowance from the other side and attach it with circular movements away from the edge of the sock. Felt both sides of the sock. With your hand inside the sock, rub the seam extensions so that they attach well.

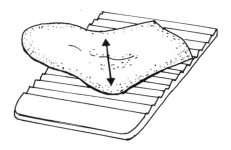

5. Full the sock using the rubbing technique. Because the sock will shrink in the direction that it is rolled and rubbed, roll it in different directions along its length and width to get even shrinkage. Shrink the ankle area by fulling diagonally, as shown.

Mittens are felted in the same way as socks. Draw a template with the thumb at a right angle to the hand. Use two layers of well-carded wool.

6. Full the sole by holding the sock as shown. Round off the corners by placing your hand in the sock and rubbing the corners against the fulling board. Or use a felting tool.

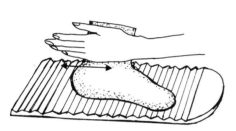

Mittens without seams.

7. To make the sock fit the foot well, score the area where the heel ends by rubbing it vigorously with the back of your hand or a felting tool.

Elephant foot or boot? A hard, totally fulled boot requires a lot of shrinkage.

8. The best way to shape the foot of the sock is to work it while it is being worn. Place the foot in a plastic bag (unless you want to wash the foot as well!) and then pull on the sock. Take care to keep the foot at a right angle from the leg so that the shaft of the sock will be perpendicular to the sole. Be careful not to make the shaft too tight.

Pattern for sewn slippers. Make the pattern larger or smaller by adjusting the sole and lengthening or shortening the back piece.

SOLE

against the sole

BACK

FRONT
BACK

CENTER
BACK

black line = sole
red line = front
blue line = back piece

Sewn Slippers and Mittens

Sew together the slipper pieces with tight blanket stitches through all layers. Use a tightly

spun yarn such as tapestry yarn. The slipper shown here was decorated with wool embroidery.

The blanket stitch will resist abrasion best if an edge of small chain stitches is crocheted over the stitches. It may be easiest to stick the crochet hook under the lower part of the stitches.

Sewn slipper. During the last stage of fulling, the felt was fulled in the washing machine to make it very dense and hard. Leather or rubber soles can be added with contact cement.

Sewn mittens

Sewn felt mittens fit well. For best results, sew them together before fulling is complete. Use a two-ply wool yarn for sewing, one that is not too tightly spun. After fulling is complete, the seams will disappear into the felt and become much tighter. The mitten on the right was sewn together and then fulled; the mitten on the left has been sewn but not yet fulled.

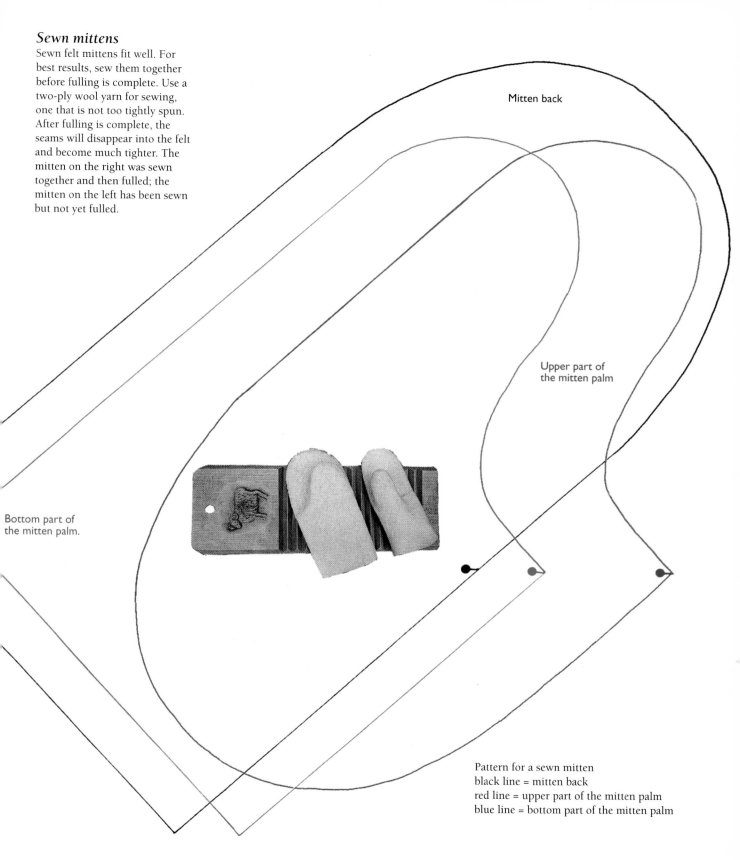

Mitten back

Upper part of the mitten palm

Bottom part of the mitten palm.

Pattern for a sewn mitten
black line = mitten back
red line = upper part of the mitten palm
blue line = bottom part of the mitten palm

Purses

Cookie-tin purse

A round purse felted on and shaped like a cookie tin, and decorated with

chain-stitch embroidery.

Metal cookie tins can give a felt purse a wonderful shape. Be sure to choose a tin that won't rust. For this purse, I sampled a carded batt of mixed wool from a large spinnery. Because I suspected that the batts contained wool from meat breeds, I added chain-stitch embroidery to help "press together" the felt and make it more stable and tight. Leicester or Swedish Fin wool of the Gobelin type would also be a suitable wool for a dressy purse. The purse required about 130 grams (4½ ounces) of wool. The tin measures 18 centimeters (7 inches) in diameter and 8 centimeters (3 inches)

A purse made similar to the cookie-tin purse but with a layer of thick foam-rubber strips wrapped around the metal container to round off the edges.

The purse with the patterned flap is made like the cookie-tin purse, but is felted around a form carved in hard foam rubber instead of a metal container. The flap is sewn on afterward. The black purse with the chain stitch embroidery is described in the text.

Felting

The purse is felted completely around the tin without leaving an opening. The opening for the zipper is cut out after felting while the tin is still inside the purse so that the purse will keep its shape. The purse can be fulled in a washing machine after being thoroughly felted. To endure rigorous use, a purse must be densely fulled.

Begin by cutting a circular template from thick plastic. The diameter of the circle should be half of the tin's depth plus the tin's diameter plus a shrinkage allowance of about 40 percent.

1. Roll out a bamboo mat. On top of the mat, lay out four crisscrossing layers of wool in the shape of the template plus about 4 centimeters (1½ inches) for a seam allowance. Sprinkle felting solution in fine drops on the wool. The surface should be covered with drops, not wet. Place the plastic template on top of the wool and fold the seam allowance right against the edge of the template. Sprinkle the seam allowance with felting solution and lightly press it down.

2. Lay out four more crisscrossing layers of wool on top of the template and covering the seam allowance. Sprinkle it with felting solution, roll up the mat together with the wool, and roll the package for about five minutes. Unroll the package, turn the purse a quarter turn, reroll it in the mat, and roll the package for another five minutes. Unroll the package, turn the purse another quarter turn. Check to make sure that there are no thin parts or "double-felted" areas that create a flap around the edge of the template. Add small bits of carded fleece to repair any thin areas that you may find. Continue rolling and twisting the purse in this way until the wool is felted.

3. Full the purse in the washing machine with 40° C (104° F) water and let it agitate for about 10 minutes, or full the purse on a felting board by hand or with more rolling. Cut an opening in the purse where the zipper will be and insert the tin. With strong thread and large basting stitches, sew the opening closed.

This will make the purse much easier to work with and will prevent the opening from deforming.

Shape the purse into the desired form by rubbing the tin and felt in all directions on a felting board. Of course, you could also rub it by hand or with a felting tool (see page 59).

When the felt feels hard and tight, wash the purse (with the tin still inside) by lifting it up and down in warm water. Let the purse air dry (with the tin still inside) and then press it with a steam iron.

If you plan to dye the purse, remove the tin, dye the purse, and then return the tin, sew the opening closed, shape the purse again, and allow it to dry.

Embroidery

Tightly spun tapestry yarn spun from long, shiny outercoat fiber makes good embroidery thread. On the cookie-tin purse, I used a shiny black synthetic knitting yarn to contrast with the black, matte felt surface.

On a piece of paper, draw a design that can be embroidered with chain stitches. Round shapes are the easiest to work; angular shapes are more complicated to sew. Apply the pattern to the felt as described in the section on marking on felt (page 100). Open the seam and remove the tin. Sew the chain-stitch embroidery from the right side of the felt. Because the fabric is tight and dense, it is not necessary to stick the needle all the way through the fabric.

Finishing

Sew a strong zipper into the opening. First, cut out a rectangular hole so that the zipper's teeth will be visible. Use button and carpet thread to sew the zipper to the purse by hand with tight hem stitches. Then tightly overcast the edges of the zipper on the inside of the purse

Make a strap from a strip of well-fulled felt. The strap should be long enough to go around the base of the purse and hang comfortably from the shoulder. Rub the strap felt crosswise (across the narrow edge) on a felting

board to make it even stronger and give it a good edge. Sew the strap to the purse or attach it with rivets or buttons. It is easiest to attach the strap with buttons; you'll need at least five. Attach the strap by sewing through the button, the strap, and the purse using button and carpet thread. If the buttons are small and match the color of the felt, they will look like rivets. If they are large or of a contrasting color, they will stand out as decoration.

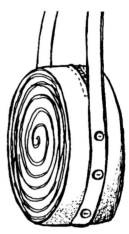

Purse with Quilting

Miklos Paiz from Ny£reghára, Hungary, calls his purse archaic and eclectic! Applied ornamentation and quilting contribute to the well-worked impression. There is a pocket inside. The wool comes from Racka sheep, an old Hungarian breed. The purse is felted in one piece around a cardboard template. The white motif on the black background is cut out of motif felt and inlaid in place. The quilting is stitched by hand with shoe thread. The eyes are enamel.

Purse with design in relief

Neo art nouveau is how Miklos Paiz describes his colorful purse made of coarse Swedish wool. The motif was inspired by the structure of the wool.

Many complicated stitches create relief in the motifs. Miklos used three methods to heighten the motifs.

1. A contour is sewn around the motif and the outside surface is "shortened" by sewing many stitches near one another.

2. To form a ridge in a motif, stitches are sewn from side to side in the motif and are pulled snugly, causing the felt to pucker into a ridge. This technique works well only for small shapes such as the ridge along the lizard's back.

3. The lizard's body is created by sewing from one side to the other and letting the thread loop under the felt on the back side. This method adds the most height to the motif.

Jewelry and Other Small Pieces

Jewelry that will be worn against the skin should be made from soft fiber such as the lamb's wool of fine-wool breeds. Jewelry can be shaped around the plastic-coated wire that is sold in spools in garden supply and hardware stores.

Felt a snake or a necklace

1. Double over a piece of plastic-coated wire. The snake's head is suggested by the fold.

2. Wind a strip of thin foam rubber around the wire to give the wool something to attach to. Secure the strip with a dab of glue or tie it in place with a piece of thread.

3. Wrap a strip of carded batt thickly around the foam rubber. Join different colors by overlapping them a centimeter (1/2 inch) or so. Dip the snake in soapy water and roll it back and forth in a bamboo mat between your palms or on a felting board. Full it until it is firm and dense so that it will not pill with use.

4. If you want the head to cross over the body, sew a little snap to the underside of the neck and the body. Make a necklace closure by making a thin felt tail over the wire on each end of the snake form. The hooks can grasp one another.

Neck bands that resemble snakes are made by felting around wire. The forms can be bent into different shapes.

Necklaces and bracelets can be made by braiding or lacing together thin strands of felt that have been rolled between the palms. The ends of the strands are formed into a button and a loop. All jewelry by Gunilla Paetau Sjöberg.

Earrings and other balls with holes. Balls with holes are made by tightly wrapping wool around a piece of doubled-over plastic-coated wire. Wrap the fleece as you would a ball of yarn. Afterward, bend the wire around the ball so that it is easier to roll the ball between your hands while you felt it. Use the fold in the wire to pull through a cord or string.

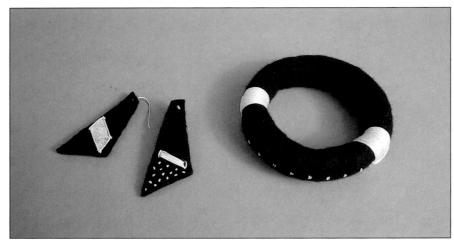

Earrings can be cut out of thin, hard felt and then embellished with simple embroidery in shiny yarn. Silver findings can be purchased at jewelry supply stores. The thick bracelet is easier to sew around a core of foam rubber (as described below) than to make as a solid felt roll. By Gunilla Paetau Sjöberg.

Strawberries on a string. Small felt balls are embroidered with small yellow-green dots and small white stitches and then threaded onto linen yarn with a felted, embroidered tip. By Gunilla Paetau Sjöberg.

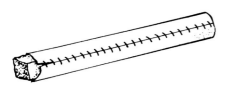

Fool your friends with a bowl of felt candies! Alternate layers of colored motif felt with black carded fleece. Felt the layers together and then cut them into strips and pieces. To help the motif felt attach to the batts, roughen up the felt surface with a steel brush. By Gunilla Paetau Sjöberg.

Sewn bracelet (shown in the photo above). Cut a narrow piece of foam rubber into a length of about 26 centimeters (10 inches) and a thickness of about 1.5 centimeters (1/2 inch). The straight sides of the foam piece will be obliterated by the felting. Cover the foam rubber with a strip of felt and stitch the long edges of the felt together. Bring the two ends of the foam rubber together and stitch the short edges of the felt tightly in place. Wet the seams with clean, warm water and felt them until the stitches disappear. Hide the join between the two ends of foam rubber with a bit of embroidery or a strip of felt in a contrasting color.

Children's Goods

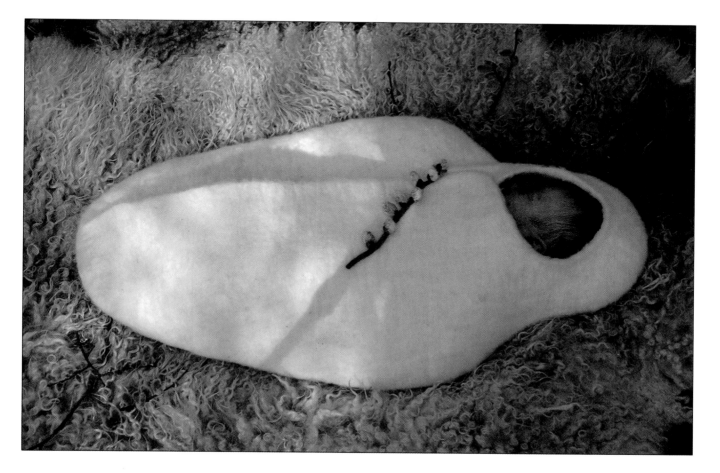

Sleep, you little willow child,
and so it is winter.
And also sleep the birch and heather,
rose and hyacinth.
And so it is long until spring,
before the mountain ash will stand in
    bloom
Sleep, you little willow,
and so it is winter.

—*Zacharias Topelius*

Throughout the ages, wool has been used to clothe children. Perhaps the inspiration for Danish felt diapers came from Turkey, where infants living in the countryside continue to be diapered in felt. Next to the body is placed a small, oblong diaper of felt on which is placed a thin felt pouch filled with sterilized clay. Around these is wrapped a triangular felt cloth followed by a felt casing. These layers of wrappings absorb moisture quickly and keep the child dry. In Mongolia, similar felt diapers are still used, but the thin felt pouch is filled with ashes from the fireplace instead of clay.

Mattress Pad

Lambskins are used to pad incubators for newborns in some Swedish hospitals. Though there may be no proven medicinal benefit, they make a soft and pleasant sleeping surface. Some hospitals use synthetic skins instead, and although they are soft, they don't have wool's ability to regulate body temperature and absorb moisture. Many hospitals choose not to use lambskins because they can not fully disinfect the skin before it is used by another infant. Disinfection is not a problem at home, where a skin is used by only one child.

Tests are presently being done to determine if lambskins can cause small children to develop allergies. Although there is very little danger of developing an allergy to wool, dust mites, which are common allergens, may nest in a pelt, especially in damp climates. But because dust mites are also present in bedcovers, carpets, and upholstery, a lambskin would pose no greater risk than a conventional bed.

An alternative to a lambskin is a felted, undyed, napped felt of the finest lamb's wool. Felt has all the qualities of a lambskin and can be washed easily. Felted wool can tolerate the high water temperatures necessary for sterilization.

Making a felt mattress pad

Lay out three to four very thick layers of carded batts from fine lamb's wool (such as Swedish Fin or Merino). Felt them moderately, wash the felt, and then brush the surface with a steel brush to form a fine, fluffy nap. To be warm, the felt should be thick and somewhat porous. Wash the pad with a mild detergent and spin out the excess water. Brush it again lightly (see the section on aftertreatments on page 79). To remove loose fibers, vacuum the pad using the curtain attachment.

Travel Pouch for Baby

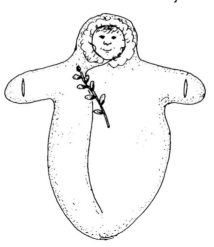

Material:

Fine lamb's wool such as Swedish Fin or Merino. For a very thick and porous winter pouch, add a thick layer of Texel wool between layers of fine wool. Texel wool will add padding, but because it will not actually felt, it will allow the pouch to remain flexible. The pouch can have an edging of washable sheepskin around the hood and a lining of cloth. You will also need a vinyl template cut roughly into the shape of an infant with outstretched arms, and a piece of plastic three-fourths as long as the template and almost as wide.

1. Felt the back side, position the template, and fold the excess fleece (seam allowances) around the template. Place the plastic on top of the piece so that it covers the right side of the pouch as shown.

2. Cover the hood area with carded batts (the hole for the face will be cut out later), as well as a little more than half of the body and the entire left side as shown. The plastic will act as a barrier and prevent this wool from attaching to the right side of the pouch.

1.

2. plastic

3. Firmly felt the wool along the opening edge. Make sure that this edge does not become felted to the seam allowances on the right side.

4. Transfer the plastic from the right to the left as shown. Cover the remaining piece with carded batts, forming a bulge at the upper edge to make a flap that can be fastened under the neck. Felt the loose fiber, including the hood. Cut a *small* hole for the face opening—it will get larger as it is fulled.

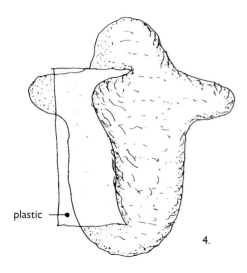

plastic

4.

5. Full, using the rolling method (see page 64). Stop fulling when the pouch is still somewhat porous, or it will not be as warm! Stretch the hood over a round form such as a ball the size of a baby's head. Felt around the edge of the face opening. Wash, brush, and vacuum the pouch.

The pouch is fastened with a "pussy willow" fastener. Make the buds by rolling small balls of gray felt, covering them with a small amount of white fleece, and rolling them again to felt the two together. Embroider the "husks" onto the right side of the felt buds using brown linen or cottolin and decorate them with yellow "pollen" embroidered with thin linen or silk thread. Sew a loop of yarn or cloth tape to the opposite side. Fasten the loop around one of the felt buds.

Danish Soaker Pants

Knitted soakers have long been common, and now felt soakers can be purchased from Kastanjehuset in Hojer, Denmark. The idea was developed by Grete Lund.

Soakers require delicate washing and can be hung to air dry if they are damp. Like knitted wool soakers, felt soakers can be rubbed with lanolin purchased from a drugstore.

The pattern is sized for a child of five to seven months.

Felting

For one pair of pants you will need about 50 grams (1¾ ounces) of carded batts. Grete uses Merino wool.

Lay out the wool in a rectangle measuring about 55 by 33 centimeters (21½ by 13 inches). Felt, using the rolling technique (see page 64). Take care that the felt shrinks equally from all directions so that the pattern will fit. When the wool is thoroughly felted, cut out the soakers according to the dimensions given. Rub the cut edges a bit to make them soft and give them a finished appearance. Wash with a mild detergent.

Sewing

Sew elastic to the waist and the leg openings using a machine zigzag stitch.

The side seams can be closed with buttons or snaps or sewn together. You can sew one side seam and put buttons or snaps on the other. When sewing, use a seam allowance of 1 centimeter (1/2 inch). Hand-sewn back stitches can also be used.

Snaps can be sewn or riveted on. Sew a cotton band behind the snaps, buttons, or buttonholes to strengthen the felt. Sew the buttons or place the snaps a little in from the side edges of the front piece so that the pants will fit snugly.

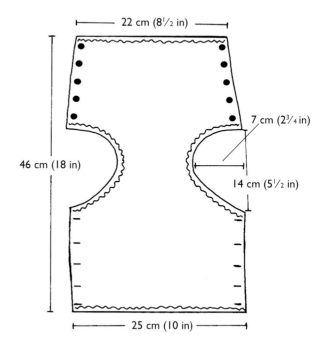

Pattern for baby shoes

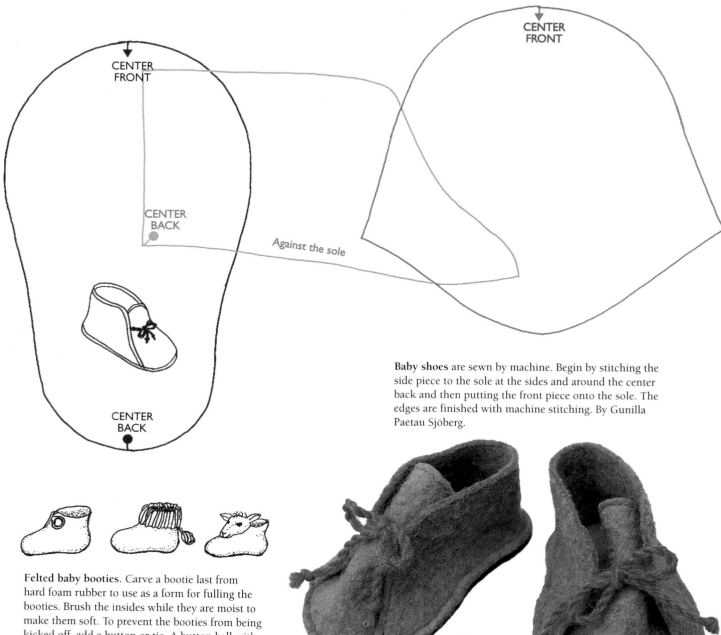

CENTER FRONT

CENTER FRONT

CENTER BACK

Against the sole

CENTER BACK

Baby shoes are sewn by machine. Begin by stitching the side piece to the sole at the sides and around the center back and then putting the front piece onto the sole. The edges are finished with machine stitching. By Gunilla Paetau Sjöberg.

Felted baby booties. Carve a bootie last from hard foam rubber to use as a form for fulling the booties. Brush the insides while they are moist to make them soft. To prevent the booties from being kicked off, add a button or tie. A button ball with a loop or a knitted ribbing are possibilities. Or sew on a felt decoration, such as a little lamb, on one side of the slit and attach it to the other side of the slit with a piece of elastic.

Can I walk with the felt boots, Grandma? wonders Alexandra, age 2, in her blueberry outfit.

The cap, which was fulled over a glass ice bucket, is trimmed with three-dimensional blueberries on a stem.

The jacket is cut from a commercial pattern, that had armholes and sleeves suitable for felt. It is edged with a dyed knitted band. The zipper pull is made from a felted blueberry.

The boots, which were fulled in the washing machine, have rubber soles glued to the bottoms and are edged with a knitted band. By Gunilla Paetau Sjöberg.

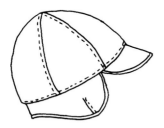

Helmet. The pieces are sewn together with button and carpet thread in blanket stitch. It is edged with a knitted band. By Gunilla Paetau Sjöberg.

The helmet can be made with a brim and edged with a strip of washable leather.

Felted Teddy Bear

This teddy bear is not the simplest to make, but it sits well and, like all felt, is washable!

Teddy bear that can sit, by Gunilla Paetau Sjöberg

Materials:

Swedish Fin wool of the Gobelin type or Gotland wool.

Felting

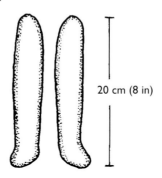

20 cm (8 in)

1. Roll carded wool into two long, somewhat thick cylinders and felt them hard on the fulling board. Lay the cylinders in an X to form the legs and arms. If the legs are too small and you are using a very fine wool, you can add onto the cylinders to make them thicker. Sometimes, I make the cylinders by rolling wool around leftover thick felt strips. You could also use old mittens or pieces of foam rubber for the inner part of the cylinders.

2. Felt two ears with fluffy wool "brushes" hanging off the bottom as shown. To make the ears, fold a small amount of wool into a sheet, leaving wisps of wool at one end. Felt the sheets between your hands with pressure, but leave the wisps unfelted.

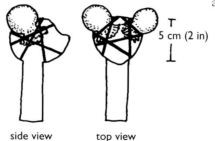

side view   top view

5 cm (2 in)

3. Using foam rubber, cut out a bear head and long neck. Position the ears with the brushes against the head. Wind carded wool around them, much like a bandage, crisscrossing the head to secure the ears. Cover the rest of the head with carded fleece. Leave the wool hanging down over the foam rubber to make a very long, sturdy neck. Felt the head firmly but don't felt the neck. Wet your fingers with felting solution while felting the head.

4. Make a tail. The tail is made the same way as the ears, only a little thicker.

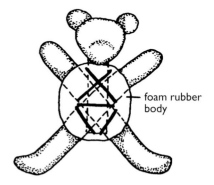

foam rubber body

5. Cross the arm and leg cylinders over the neck. Use wool yarn to hold the pieces together as shown. Lay a wool ball or a rounded piece of foam rubber on the abdomen and wind a carded fleece "bandage" around the entire works for the body. When you have wrapped almost as much wool as you want for the body, position and secure the tail as you did the ears. Moisten and rub all of the loose areas. Felt hard so that the bear will not collapse when squeezed.

6. Wash the bear, spin out the water, and let it dry sitting in the desired position. Use wool yarn to embroider eyes and a nose.

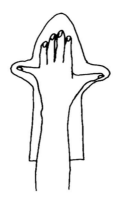

1. Draw a rough pattern of your hand while holding out your thumb and little finger as shown.

Hand puppet, by Gudrun Käll. The head is made as described for the teddy bear on page 124. To fit the fingers into the head, a hole was carved in the foam rubber head/neck piece. The body was attached to the neck during felting.

Hand puppet with an open mouth. Gotland wool is ideal for this mouse puppet because it is easy to shape. Swedish Fin wool mixed with Rya is a good alternative. By Gunilla Paetau Sjöberg.

2. Using pictures of mice as a guide, draw exaggerated features on the pattern—long nose, ears, and eyes—to give the puppet character.

3. Make a revised pattern that allows for ease of movement and shrinkage, about 3 centimeters (1 1/4 inches). Cut the larger pattern out of bubble wrap or thick plastic to make a template.

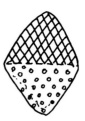

4. Draw a pattern for a double mouth with each side as long as the nose. Lay out two layers of wool, felt them lightly, and cut out the mouth shape, following the pattern.

5. Felt two ears, leaving a small, dry brush of wool on each so that they can be felted onto the body.

6. Lay out the front side of the mouse by positioning eyes and nose on the work surface, followed by layers of carded batts that allow for an ample seam allowance. Place the template on top of the wool and felt the pattern area, being careful to keep the seam allowance dry. Fold the dry seam allowance over the template and moisten it to hold the wool in place.

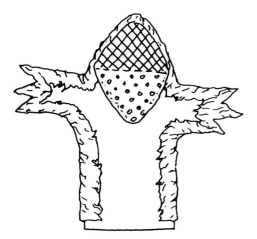

7. Position the mouth in place. Felt the upper half of the mouth (to the foldline) to the seam allowance.

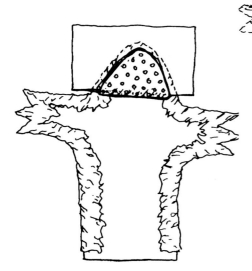

8. Lay a piece of plastic on the upper part of the mouth so that the lower edge of the plastic is aligned with the fold in the mouth. Fold the mouth over the plastic as shown.

9. Position the carded batts, decorations, and ears for the back of the mouse. You do not need to allow for another seam extension if you took care to lay out the wool evenly on the front side. Place a thin piece of plastic under the ears so that they do not become felted to the body. Felt the body, adding a tail if desired.

10. Shape the mouse on your hand, using a felting board or felting tool. Full the underside of the chin so that the nose peeks out in front. Shape the head, nose, and paws. Sew on details such as mohair whiskers. Sew on teeth made of hard felt. Squeak!

An easier way to make an open mouth is to felt the mouse without the mouth, but do not full it entirely. Then cut the hole for the mouth and sew in a piece of felt for the inner mouth. Continue fulling. The stitches will disappear into the felt, making the seams invisible when the fulling is complete.

Felt for the Home

The rolling technique allows large projects such as interior textiles to be made from felt. Wool felt has many of the qualities desired in household textiles: it reduces noise, creates a sense of warmth and coziness, and doesn't attract dust in the same way that synthetic material does. Wool requires less frequent washing than other materials, and it is less likely to stain.

Of considerable importance is that wool felt is considered fireproof. Under controlled tests, a piece of wool felt artwork was shown to self-extinguish after being exposed to an open flame for fifteen to twenty seconds.

Seat Cushions

For many years, I've sat at my drawing table on a chair padded with a felt cushion made of soft Rya wool. Over the years, the cushion has become somewhat flatter and shinier. The sheen may be a result of the wool scales wearing down. Otherwise, it looks much as it did when it was new, even the inlaid design of cut Gotland felt remains clear.

Look to the Mongolian undyed carpets with their tight, quilted patterns for ideas on how to decorate and strengthen seat cushions. Another idea is to felt plaited felt strips to a layer of wool, which will also produce a thick, strong cushion.

If you want to make a spongy cushion, add a thick layer of a nonfelting wool such as Texel between layers of good felting wool, and felt them together. The nonfelting wool will remain elastic and springy and form a stuffing between two layers of felt. Stitch the layers together for a quilted effect.

John Kandell's chairs, Camilla, with felted seat cushions by Gunilla Paetau Sjöberg. **Seat Cushions** of Gobelin wool. The center design of the cushion on the right is machine-quilted. The center design of the cushion on the left is made of felt strips woven in a tabby weave and then fulled. On both cushions, the center design is framed by couched cord and strips of felt that have been sewn around the felt.

Pillow, by Britt-Mari Hellgren. The fabric is Swedish Fin wool felted in the rolling technique using a rag rug for the support cloth. The design was cut out of prefelted fabric and felted onto the background wool. Fine tassels of dyed horsehair are sewn into the corners.

Carpets

Felt carpets date back to antiquity. They are insulating, abrasion resistant, and not especially difficult to make. Look at the section on traditional felt carpets in different lands (pages 29–36), with its many examples of working methods and designs, for inspiration.

Design and materials

Make your first felted carpet a small one so that you can sample the techniques. You can choose, for example, to work in dyed fleece or motif felt. Or try both techniques in the same carpet to get a feel for the effects they produce.

Museums hold a wealth of design inspirations. Study artifacts of wood and bark, their painted, chipped, and carved patterns. These as well as plaiting patterns can be easily adapted for use in felt. Read the section on felting designs (pages 68–72) for instructions on working with motifs.

Laying out the wool

To begin, place the carded fleece on top of a large piece of cotton cloth, such as a bedsheet, moistened with felting solution. Fold the edges of the cloth toward the center of the fleece before rolling it up to make the edges of the carpet firm and straight.

You do not need to prepare the layers of carded batts with the same precision required for other felt projects. Because there are so many layers of fleece in a carpet, a thick or thin spot in one layer will not be evident in the finished piece.

If you will be stacking a very thick pile of carded fleece, put small horizontal folds in the cloth support material before placing the wool on it. The folds will stretch out as the wool/cloth packet is rolled up, preventing the fleece from folding in on itself. You may also want to begin rolling with a large-diameter rolling bar and change to a smaller one after the layers have compacted a bit.

Roll-up Curtains, by Pia Wallén. Felt and fulling has long interested the designer**Pia Wallén** of Stockholm. Her designs for industry have take many forms, from clothing to interior textiles. An example is the woven and fulled blanket, *Cross*, which lies on the bed in a house in Gotland. The sweater that Pia is wearing was knitted and then fulled. Pia has studied felt as a handcraft in different cultures with the emphasis on its form and function. The roll-up curtains hanging in the window are also made of felt. Pia says:

I was inspired by the nomadic use of felt. For example, in a yurt, the door can be rolled up and down or a section of the wall can be rolled out of the way. This is both practical and beautiful. Felt is a

ancient material, and it is thrilling to see what can be done with it in the 1990s. Ecological considerations are important. It is necessary to take both the environment and people's needs into account when designing for production.

The curtains are simple and functional. The felt filters the light pleasantly and is a fine contrast to the plastered stone walls. In addition, felt offers good insulation against drafts from the window and the winter chill. These curtains are made from industrial felt, but flexible handmade felt could also be used. The curtains are held in place with narrow felt bands and are attached to the wall with metal buttons fastened through grommets.

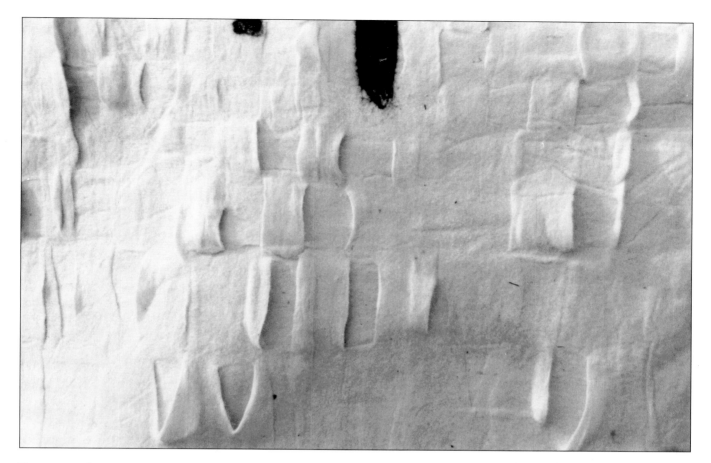

Hans-Dieter Klotz is somewhat of a rarity, a male felt artist. He lives in Germany, but it was at a workshop on the Hungarian pusta, that I saw Hans-Dieter and his wife weave this soft lap robe from Merino wool tops. Tops (the thick and ropelike fiber preparation for commercial spinning of yarn, also called roving), can be purchased from a spinnery or from most fiber supply stores.

The tops were woven in tabby weave; alternate "warps" of roving were lifted, and rows of weft roving were laid in place. Then the fibers were felted together with the rolling technique. The tabby-weave structure formed two wool layers that attached to each other where they crossed. The woven structure is visible in the finished lap robe.

For best results, position the design motifs upside down on the support material before laying out the wool. If the motifs are placed on top of a high pile of wool, they will shift considerably during felting and fulling, and their definition may be lost. If you use motifs made of loose wool, pieces should be thick enough to prevent the background wool from showing through and obliterating the design. If you use motifs made of prefelted pieces, baste them together with thread where they touch one another so that they will not shift when the piece is rolled. The stitches can be picked out after the felt is well formed.

Choose a strong, abrasion-resistant wool such as Rya or Gotland for the rug. If you use Rya, the layer next to the motifs should be a mixture of equal parts Rya and Swedish Fin wool so that the design will adhere better. Pure Rya will not adhere well to the motif felt.

For a thick carpet, stack many layers of carded fleece. The felt will be stronger if it is made from many thin layers of fleece placed at right angles to one another than if only one or two thick layers are used. If you must use inferior wool, put it in the middle layers where it will be surrounded by good wool.

Carpet of stick-beaten Gute wool. The design was taken from a butter mold at the history museum in Sveg. Made in a felting course at the Bäckedal Folk High School, 1991.

Felting

1. Sprinkle the wool with a felting solution that contains extra soap. Use fine drops; too much water will cause creases to form. Fold the edges of the support cloth over the long outside edges of the carpet fleece. Beginning at one short end, roll the fleece and support cloth around a rolling bar. Rolling the thick packet can be cumbersome; you may need someone to help. Carefully stretch the support cloth as you roll the packet as tightly as possible. There probably will be folds in the sheet that will not smooth out entirely the first time you roll the packet. The folds will make thin stripes in the wool that should be smoothed out after each rolling. Thump firmly across the roll with your hands to help remove some of the air.

2. Roll the packet back and forth for 10 to 15 minutes to remove the air from the wool. At first, the roll will feel limp, but it will firm up as air escapes. Carefully unroll the packet. Do not be distressed if motifs stick to the support cloth instead of the wool. They will adhere to the wool as the felting progresses. Without separating it from the wool, straighten out any creases in the cloth and adjust the edges so that they are straight. Carefully pull on the wool so that both short edges are even. The upper layer of the wool will tend to slide over the lower layer in the direction in which the packet is rolled and must be pulled back into place. Sprinkle the wool with more fine drops of felting solution and then reroll the packet, this time from the other short side. Roll the packet back and forth for another 10 to 15 minutes.

3. Continue rolling, unrolling, sprinkling, and rerolling in the opposite direction until the carpet wool is flat and thoroughly damp. Adjust the edges between rollings by tugging on areas that have drawn in and pushing in any areas that have spread out. Also straighten the carpet wool in all directions and adjust the position of the design motifs if necessary, using a large, sharp needle to adjust them. The motifs are most easily pulled

Carpet with its inspiration: a bark basket from the history museum in Sveg. The light areas were cut out of prefelted pieces and then felted together with dark brown batts. The small felt appliqué work was sewn in place with yarn before the piece was felted. Made in a felting course at Bäckedal Folk High School, 1991.

into position in the early stages of rolling.

4. When the design motifs have adhered to the felt, you can stop using the rolling bar. At this point, turn over the wool and roll the wool/support packet with the design facing upward so that it will be on the inner curve of the roll. This will make the design flatter against the background felt. A carpet must be fulled very firmly if it is to be walked on, so work until it is very stiff.

5. Wash, straighten, and adjust the edges of the carpet while it is damp. With a thick, sharp needle, adjust the details of the design, such as the corners, so that they are even and pleasing. The edges of the carpet can be evened out by rubbing them with felting tools and tugging on them to straighten and block their shape.

Laying out the round carpet. A mirror image of the design (worked of pencil roving and cut felt pieces) was positioned on top of the support cloth, as was a border of black, carded batts. Afterward, stick-beaten Gute wool was placed over the design in the Mongolian method (see page 25.)

Fulling the carpet back and forth using the rolling technique is an opportunity for close personal contact!

Round carpet inspired by a lid for a round box, shown by happy course participants.

Maisa Tikkanen of Finland is working on a line of production carpets with a felt factory. She does the first stage of felting in her own studio and the heavy fulling at the factory.

Teaching Feltmaking

Felting with Children

Childhood's finest
and perhaps solely indisputable benefits
are the sensory awareness,
the spontaneity,
the unspoiled eye,
the barefooted communion with nature.

—*Werner Aspenström*

The process of feltmaking can teach children many things.

Sensory experiences

Children should fully experience wool: smell the odor of the sheep barn and the wool, hear the sheep's bleat, look into the sheep's yellow eyes, race small lambs on wobbly legs, feel wavy tufts of wool on a warm sheep's body, the lanolin and softness of the wool. These experiences are valuable to children who spend much of their time in front of the television, videos, and computer games. Although sensory experiences are important for childhood development, most children don't get much sensory experience at school.

Imagination and creativity

Wool offers a wealth of opportunity for developing the imagination and creativity. Even very young children can felt small shapes. These shapes are easy to work with: to sew into, to wear, to join together. The imagination is given room to play, and creative solutions are encouraged. Practical and whimsical projects require problem-solving skills.

Material knowledge and consumer aspects

Sheep breeds, types of wool, their suitability for different purposes, how wool should be washed, ways to prevent shrinkage, and more: all are made evident through the process of felting. A sense for quality and craftsmanship is also developed, from choosing the wool and felting technique to using the finished product. After wearing a pair of felted socks, for example, the choices made in wool selection, felting technique, and degree of fulling can be evaluated.

Integration with other subjects

A knowledge of mathematics is required to figure percentages for dyeing or shrinkage. A social awareness comes with learning about felt in terms of culture, history, environmental concerns, and energy supplies.

Jan with his sheep. It is easy to embroider on felt!

Energy supplies and the economy

By wearing a wool sweater and a pair of felt socks, you can save energy by lowering the household temperature by at least 1°C (about 1/2°F) .Your energy savings will be about 5 percent. Imagine the savings for a family over the course of a year! Imagine the savings if every household did this!

Allergies and Asthma

Because many children have some form of allergy, before you plan a lesson using unwashed wool, find out if any children in the group have allergies to unwashed wool and read the section on allergies and other problems (see page 53). Because allergens can remain in the air, find out if anyone with allergies will be using the room after you.

It is important for all children to have a chance to participate, so you may choose to work only with wool that has been thoroughly prewashed. Well-washed wool poses no more allergy danger than a common wool sweater. Wash the wool in many baths, rinse it carefully, and spin out the water between rinsings. Alternatively, use finished batts or wool from a commercial carding company that washes its wool well. If the wool is dyed, it can be considered clean.

Equipment and Materials

Make a simple felting table by taping newspaper rolls to the edges of a table and covering it with plastic as described on page 57. (Push several tables together to work large pieces.) The children can stand around the table and be sloppy without the floor's getting overly wet. Have plenty of rags and buckets on hand for cleanup. If you use the rolling technique, you can omit the newspaper rolls and just cover the table with plastic.

For felting trays, use plastic storage trays or cafeteria food trays. A simple, small felting tray can be made of a garbage bag that has been cut open and flattened, with the corners paper-clipped together to make a raised edge. Balls can be felted in a dishpan.

Fulling boards are not always necessary. Small felt pieces, such as those used as a background for embroidery, can be fulled simply by rolling them up and then squeezing the roll. Bamboo window shades or placemats can be used with the rolling technique for items that need more fulling. Felt socks need to be fulled firmly on a fulling board. Lay the board on a terry-cloth towel on the felting table to prevent the board from slipping. If you don't have a fulling board, use a wooden plank with rope wrapped around it.

Uncarded Wool versus Carded Batts

When felting with children, you can use either uncarded wool or carded batts purchased from a commercial carding company. If allergies are an issue, purchased carded batts are a convenient solution that have the added advantages of being easy to store and free of dirt, waste material, and smell. They also eliminate the time-consuming task of carding. On the other hand, carded batts do not provide the full felting experience, and the children will have less exposure to the differences between breeds, their wool types, and characteristics.

To stick-beat wool like the Mongolians is a fun diversion to the usual school day. You can use a tarp instead of an old felt as the Mongolians do.

By rolling the felt outdoors on a warm day, children can quickly make a large felt for embroidery and other projects. A discarded shade was used here for its last duty.

Teasing wool is not so easy if the wool staple is long! Pull the wool out by its width, not its length.

Felting with Young Children

Even very young children can make felt. Three-year-olds can roll a small amount of wool in their hands, and to their great surprise, discover that it turns into a little ball! For beginning projects, try three-dimensional felting, worked between the hands with motions that are familiar to children. Flat projects can be more difficult because they require more developed fine motor skills. The small lumps and balls the children produce will awaken their imagination and associations!

To teach the children where wool comes from, take them (the nonallergic ones!) to a farm where they can mingle with the sheep, feel their fleeces, and watch the sheep get sheared.

Teasing Wool

It can be difficult for small children to maneuver a pair of heavy hand carders. Instead, let them tease the wool by pulling the wool staple apart with their fingers. Swedish Fin wool of the Gobelin type or Gotland wool responds well to this treatment. Hold up a wool staple that has a shape resembling an icicle and explain how the icicle should be fluffed up to form a summer cloud! Demonstrate how the wool is pulled apart, fiber by fiber, until the tuft is totally fluffed. Then demonstrate how the same effect is achieved with hand carders.

Working with Teased Wool

For a first project, make a felt ball. Begin by winding the teased wool into a firm ball, and hold the ball so that the wool can not unwind. Exaggerate the importance of the movements to impress upon the children how it should be done. Dip the ball into a bowl of felting solution that contains a lot of soap. Roll the ball around and around between your palms until the wool holds together.

If the "ball" becomes oblong or pointed, encourage the child to imagine what the wool is trying to form: a mouse, a seal, a shark, a fish, a bird? A fold in the ball can become a mouth; a protruding flap, or maybe a tongue!

Give the felted shape some color by winding it with some colored carded fleece. Wind a little fuzzy yarn around the ball to hold the batting together while adding decoration. Dip the ball in felting solution and roll it between the hands again. A multicolored ball can be made by winding on different colors in the same way.

For best results, begin with small balls that fit inside the children's hands. Later, the balls can be made bigger by adding more carded fleece. Have the children wash the balls in lukewarm water with a little dish detergent and then rinse them well. If a centrifuge or washing machine is available, use it to spin out the water. Lay the balls on newspapers to air dry.

Balls, Easter eggs, rats, hedgehogs, whales, and fish are just some of the things that can be made from a ball.

"Finnish Sticks"

After making balls, teach the children to make "Finnish sticks" (felted wool snakes). Begin by winding wool into a hard roll. Felt the roll by rolling it back and forth between the palms. Snakes, worms, and electric eels will suddenly appear! Make tails by rolling very thin strips of wool.

Forming Animals from Parts

An animal can be made by felting rods or cylinders for legs and a ball for the body. Ears can be made by folding in the edges of small bits of wool and rubbing them between the hands. Use scissors to shorten legs, make ears smaller, and make cloven hooves. The felted pieces can be sewn together, eyes embroidered, and hair sewn on.

As they gain experience, the children can try to felt the various parts together instead of sewing them. Let them begin by felting a tail to the body of a felted animal. Show them how to leave a "brush" of dry wool on pieces to be felted to another and how to wind wool around the brush to secure the piece in place.

Once they know how to felt balls, sticks, and flat pieces, and how to join these shapes to one another, children can create their own fantasies. Let them experiment!

Can it really be a ball of wool? wonder the girls in Tummelisa preschool in Gävle. A plastic storage box can be used to keep water off the tabletops. Because a sprinkling bottle can be difficult for small hands to handle, put the felting solution in a bowl.

Small teddy bears made by sewing together balls and "Finnish sticks". Anna-Lena Carlberg's preschool students furnished the teddy bears with different accessories.

Gray rats search for a piece of cheese.

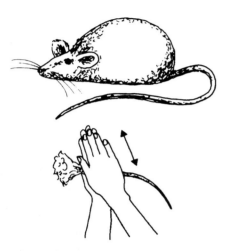

The **rat with a felted-in tail** teaches the finer points of felting.

1. Make the tail first by dipping a strip of carded wool into felting solution and rubbing it between the palms. Leave a dry brush of wool on one end.

2. Roll a strip of carded wool around the dry part of the tail and keep wrapping it to form a ball. Dip it in felting solution and roll the ball around and around between the palms. Shape the rat's nose by pinching the ball between the thumb and the forefinger and twisting it into a point.

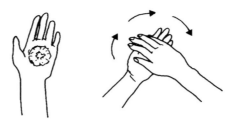

3. Make ears by folding in the edge of a thin piece of carded wool, moistening it with felting solution, and pressing it firmly while rubbing it back and forth between the palms. Sew the ears in place on the head.

Felted Sheep on a Wool Background. This method can be used for all animals or other motifs which can be assembled from felted parts. Lay out at least two layers of carded wool for a background. Sprinkle felting solution in the middle of the wool and press it down. The sheep will adhere to the middle of this background during felting. Make legs by rolling carded wool into rods (see page 83). Dip them in felting solution and roll them between the hands. Leave a fluffy brush on one end so that the legs can be joined to the body. Ears and tails are made in the same way, only smaller.

Fold carded wool into a head and neck, leaving a fluffy dry wool brush on the end of the neck. Dip the head in felting solution and place it on top of the ears' brushes. Lay out wool staple in rows, with the staple aligned vertically to the height of the body. Use plenty of wool to give the sheep a full body. To prevent the sheep from moving, place a thin, wet sheet of plastic on top of the wool as you work. Turn the work over and rub over the spot where the sheep is on the right side to help it adhere to the background. Full by kneading the felt roll by hand. Tug on the legs, head and ears after washing to shape them. You may also carefully cut them as needed. Fluff up the locks with a large, sharp needle.

After they gain a little experience, show the children how to put the parts together by preparing legs and tails with dry wool brushes, folding a little wool into a head, making small rods for the ears and position their dry wool brushes on the back of the head, folding a large package of wool for the body, placing it on top of all of the brushes, pouring felting solution over the entire works, and rubbing the animal carefully. To keep the pieces in place, cover the wool with a thin sheet of plastic. Pour more felting solution on top of the plastic to lubricate it and make it easier to rub. Teach the children to rub very lightly in small circles from the outer edges inward to the center of the body. Lift up the plastic to straighten the pieces as needed.

TOP: Monsters are popular even with high schoolers. They can be made flat or as hand puppets.

LEFT: No two sheep are alike when children do their own interpretations.

Felting a Hand-Puppet Monster

The beginner will have good luck making a puppet from Gotland wool, which felts easily. Use Rya and Spelsau wool for decoration.

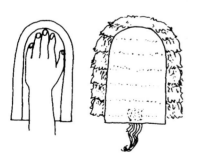

1. Read about three-dimensional felting on page 74. Prepare the body of the puppet by laying out at least two layers of wool for the back side plus a lock of wool for the tail. Note: make the seam allowance 4 to 5 centimeters (1^1/$_2$ to 2 inches) wider than the template on both sides and the top. The template should stick out at the bottom. Felt the wool slightly.

2. Fold the seam allowance over the template and moisten it with felting solution so that it stays in place. Position felt for hair, arms, and legs as desired. Arms and legs can be made in the same way as the "Finnish sticks" on page 135.

3. Add two crisscrossing layers of wool for the front side as you did for the back side, but do not make a seam allowance. Form a face by folding under the edges of a flat sheet of wool and positioning it on the front side of the puppet. Roll two small bits of wool into eyes.

Make a nose by folding a piece of wool many times. Make a mouth by rolling a thin string of wool between your palms. Place a thin sheet of plastic over the puppet so that the pieces will stay in place as you begin felting. Press the added features down into the wet wool. If they are not moistened enough, lift the plastic and add more felting solution. When the front is felted, turn the puppet over and felt the other side. Place your hand inside the puppet and felt the seam allowance to the front edge. Full the puppet by kneading the felt roll by hand.

Felting Sheets for Embroidery

A piece of felted fabric can make a fine background for embroidery. Felt is easy to stitch into, and no embroidery hoop is required to stretch the material. Shapes cut from felt will not ravel.

Instruct the children to stack enough layers to make a thick piece of felt that will be rigid and easy to handle. If the felt is too thin, the embroidery stitches will cause puckers.

If the rolling technique is used, a number of felt sheets can be made at the same time. Begin by spreading out a large bamboo window shade on the worktable. Assign each child a position at the table to lay out a square of carded fleece, about three layers thick. Depending on the dimensions of the shade, all of the squares can be worked at once. (An alternative is to lay out the wool over the entire bamboo shade, felt it as single large sheet, and then cut it into pieces.) This method is convenient if you work with commercially carded batts or large, drum-carded batts. The edges of cut pieces can be smoothed out by rubbing them after they are cut. The rolling technique is simple, it doesn't cause a flood of water, and children enjoy taking turns rolling the packet. Put a smooth, rubber-backed throw rug underneath the roll so that it won't slide across the floor. To produce very tight and firm squares, knead them in a little warm felting solution in a bucket or dishpan after they have been rolled. Embroider with two-ply wool yarn.

Learning about Wool Types

Even if it's not possible to visit a sheep farm, learning about wool can be exciting. Before the children arrive, place a bag of assorted types of fleece in the middle of the floor and illuminate it with a lamp. The effect will be most dramatic

"My favorite animal" is a popular theme for embroidering on felt. Here is a dwarf rabbit!

on an autumn afternoon when the sun is dim and all other electric lights are turned off. When the children enter the room, instruct them to close their eyes and put their hands into the mysterious bag to feel its contents and to smell its odor.

Then empty the wool onto the floor and allow the children to dive down into the wool and search for as many different types of staples as they can find. Arrange the staples in a row—black, brown, gray, and white, long and short, coarse and fine, wavy and straight, shiny and matte. They will soon understand that all wool is not the same, that it comes in many varieties with unique characteristics, and that if there are differences among wool, there must be differences among sheep as well.

Cutouts of various breeds of sheep are paired with wool staples.

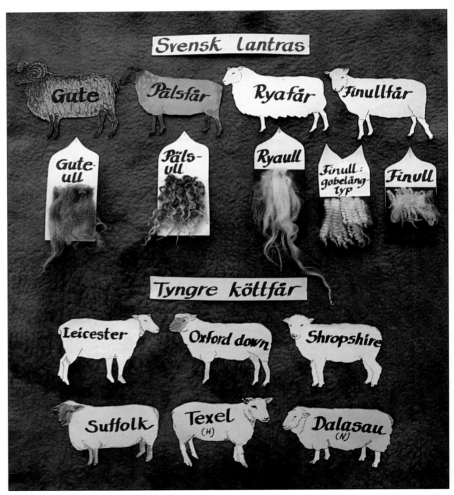

Learning about Wool Characteristics

Compare the coarseness of the various staples, how they feel against the face. Discuss why some sheep have both outercoats and undercoats, how that benefits the sheep, and how they can be used to their best advantage. Look, feel, and squeeze the different fleeces and finished items made from them. Compare and study. What characteristics should wool garments have? What characteristics should a neck scarf have? Felt socks? What type of wool should be chosen for each? The discussion should include such characteristics as durability, warming ability, and softness.

Drop a dirty wool tuft into a bowl of warm water. Watch as it turns white and clean and the water turns brown. Discuss how the sheep makes its own soap from lanolin and sweat. Nature makes its own small wonders!

Next, watch what happens when the wool is rolled up, dipped in warm felting solution, and rubbed between the hands. Watch as it shrinks into a small, tight ball, and the fibers attach tightly to one another. This tells the exciting tale about the little wool fiber. If the fleece has long fiber, rub it into a snake shape. Explore how much more easily the fiber can shrink if it is lubricated with felting solution. Explain how the fiber locks together with shrinkage and cannot be pulled apart.

As you discuss what happens during the felting process, explain why a wool sweater shrinks when washed in a washing machine. Teach the children how to correctly wash a wool garment so that it won't shrink. Undoubtedly, someone will argue that some wool sweaters can be washed in the machine. Take this opportunity to describe Superwash and other treatments that erode the scales on the fibers with chemicals or cover them with a thin resin so that they cannot migrate and therefore cannot felt.

Stone Sheep, by Lillian Widgren-Jacobsson. Wind carded wool around a stone. Felt. The head is felted as an egg-shaped ball. Ears are sewn on. The bodies of some of the sheep in this picture are knitted from handspun yarn.

Felting other things

Imagination and the pleasure of discovery will know no bounds when the felter realizes that other fibers such as flax, silk and cotton can be felted into the wool. Or pieces of felt, cloth, threads, yarns, grass, and hair of all types! Or that the wool can be dyed uncarded or as carded fibers or as finished cloth.

Pieces of felt cloth

Pieces of felt can be used in many ways. They can be cut up and sewn into slippers for Grandmother, animals, notebook covers, finger puppets, hand puppets, masks, doll clothing, tea cozies, purses, needle cases, soles, seat cushions, hot pads, oven mitts, mittens, caps, shoes, and much more.

An unsuccessful or lonely felt sock can make a fine broomstick sheep. Sew on ears and a "genuine" mock pelt (see page 73).

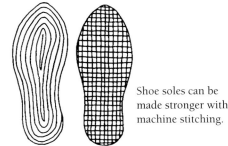

Shoe soles can be made stronger with machine stitching.

Fredrik, sixteen, felted a pair of felt boots as a present for his girlfriend.

A beginner's handspun yarn is dyed with lichens and crocheted into a body for Ruffe the fox. The nose and ears are sewn from small felt pieces that were dyed in the same dyebath.

For felt pieces that need to be shaped, such as hair bands, earmuffs, and animal tails, place several plastic-covered wires in one of the layers of batts.

Group Work with Children

Most public schools do not provide many opportunities for group work on a single project. Felting a large project, such as a carpet or wall hanging, provides an exception. Students can gather around a large table equipped with a rolled-newspaper edge and covered with a sheet of plastic. Everyone can help lay out the composition and begin to rub it. Then comes the fun and popular task of fulling. The children can roll the large felt roll back and forth under their forearms or feet while singing a song to help them keep the rhythm!

Project "Home District" in Hökhuvud

About sixty children go to the *Reuterskiöldska* school in northern Hökhuvud.

As a centennial present for the school, the community financed the cost of a wall hanging to be made for the school cafeteria. The wall hanging was made as a joint project between the students and an artist (me!).

Planning

I first met with the teachers to discuss the planning, allergic children (there weren't any!), work space, division of labor, organization, and equipment.

Because none of the children had felted before, I began with an inspirational lecture and showed typical Swedish felt items, both large and small. Then I showed slides from feltmaking sessions and felt culture in Central Asia to give the children an understanding of how people make felt and the role that felt plays in the lives of nomads. We also looked at pictures of felt art made by both children and adults.

We then discussed possible compositions for a large cartoon that the students would design and paint in art class and then recreate with felt. We settled on a simple composition of the children's own environment: the landscape they saw outside their school. There were autumn leaves, black fields, a tractor, and horses in a pasture. Happily, the autumn colors were ones that would coordinate best with the warm color scheme in the school cafeteria.

We also talked about how the students should design the cartoon. They would begin with crayons and use watercolors for the large areas. They would avoid fussy details that would be impossible to achieve in felt.

The design

The finished cartoon included horses, a moose, and large, lovely leaves. I assembled all of the motifs in the cartoon on a large piece of paper and photocopied them so that the originals would not be destroyed when the children cut out the individual motifs. Some small motifs were enlarged several times on a photocopier, so that they would be easier to cut out.

I dyed the wool and carded batts to match the children's designs; it wasn't possible to dye at the school.

The big felting day

All of the tables in the cafeteria were stacked to make room for the 1.6-by-6.5-meter (5¼-by-21¼-foot) project. We made a felting table by attaching newspaper rolls to the edge of a giant table and covering it with plastic.

We nailed the large cartoon to the wall. I explained how I had laid out their pictures and how the foreground and background had different details and simplifications.

The children were divided into six groups; each included some older children, who would help the younger ones. The tasks were divided among the six groups: the leaves that were to be in the borders at each end; the tractors and clock tower; the church and cemetery; the horses, cats, and rat; the trees in the foreground, sheep, and moose; and the remaining trees and grave mound in the background. To avoid confusion, the children wore labels identifying which group they belonged to.

Motif felts

Motif felts—the church, the tractor, the moose, etc.—were made first. Carded batts were laid out in two layers on a bamboo mat. The wool was sprinkled with felting solution and rolled up. Then some of the students sat and rolled the mat under their feet.

When the felt was somewhat hard, the students cut out the shapes, beginning with the ones photocopied from the cartoon. Cutting out the paper first helped them to get a feel for the shape of a motif. The paper patterns were pinned to the motif felt and the shapes cut out.

Laying out the wool and details

We began by laying out two thick layers of carded batts of white Swedish Fin wool of the Gobelin type for the back side. Then we added thick clumps of dyed batts: brownish black for the fields, brownish beige blended with bits of green for the dry grass, and dark greenish blue for the end borders.

After the details had been prepared, they were assembled. The leaves were positioned and decorated with small pieces of cut felt to match the painted flecks in the cartoon. Small pieces were added to resemble small, falling leaves. Treetops were made from uncarded wool staples in pretty autumn colors; trunks were cut out of felt. The branches were made of felt rolled between the palms. Two small girls became the sheep experts: they rolled rods for the legs and

ears, leaving dry, bushy ends that could be joined to the other body parts, used uncarded white wool for the pelts, and a bit of folded wool for the heads. A boy who helped his father tend the shrubs in the churchyard became another expert. He cut out the fine windows, door, and even different types of gravestones. Surfaces that touched were brushed up to give them enough free fiber to attach to each other. Two students were dubbed the "soap slaves". Their job was to provide a plentiful supply of warm felting solution.

The felting solution was applied by splashing it over the children's opened hands so that it spread out in droplets. A thin sheet of plastic was placed on top of the wool to prevent the loose details from slipping out of place. The children then used their hands to press down on top of the plastic to push the air out of the wool. Then a small amount of felting solution was poured on top of the plastic, and the children rubbed on top of the plastic. This method is ideal for beginners because everyone can work his or her own area, and if anything goes wrong, the plastic can be lifted up and the wool adjusted. When the wool had felted well to itself, the plastic was removed, and the children continued to work circular motions with their hands directly on the wool.

Because there was not space for all sixty children at the table at the same time, they took turns. The children who were not working at the felting table learned how to card and to spin on a spindle.

Fulling

The last event of the day was fulling. The children enjoyed rolling the felt into a giant sausage and then rolling it back and forth on the table. We sang such songs as "Baa, Baa, Black Sheep" and a version of "Now Shall We Full the Felt Today".

We chanted the word "felt" in ten different languages as we rolled. The felt was rolled in turn from all four sides to keep the shrinkage even.

The decorations are laid out and the wool is sprinkled with felting solution.

Many different colors are needed for the picture. The wool for the motifs that are to be cut out is laid on a bamboo mat, moistened, and then lightly felted.

Felting with the rubbing technique. A thin plastic sheet placed on top of the wool prevents the motifs from shifting under eager fingers. Felting solution is sprinkled on top of the plastic to help the fingers glide well.

The patterns are placed on top of the pieces of motif felt, and the motifs are cut out.

When it was finished, the felt was carried to the school yard in a large tub. And then came the exciting moment when we got to see the completed project (see page 132)—it turned out well, don't you think?

Mounting

After the piece had been washed and dried, it was mounted. Common curtain pleating tape was sewn onto the upper edge, and hooks were threaded into the band in several places. Later, nails were put into the wall to hold the piece.

Evaluation

Doing so much work in one day was difficult. It would have been much easier to have spread it out over two days so that a day could have been devoted exclusively to laying out the composition and felting it. It would have also helped to have had the children practice making a small piece of felt before beginning the large work.

But even though the children were bombarded with a huge amount of information in a short time, they thoroughly enjoyed working together to create something tangible. They all left with the understanding that it took all 120 of their hands to create the impressive hanging in a single day.

The piece is fulled by being rolled with pressure along its length and width. Then the roll was carried out to the school yard, opened up, and the felt was held up for admiration! (See page 132.)

Storytelling Yurt

Stephanie Bunn, from West York in England, is an environmental sculptor, feltmaker, and researcher of Central Asiatic tents. She has built two storytelling yurts with children. Inside the yurts, children tell stories to each other, sing, listen to fables and tales, and read.

The large projects required three assistants: an artist, a storyteller, and a singer. Ninety children from three different schools participated in the work. Stephanie relates:

We began with a look at Yevgheny Sorokin's book *The Kirghiz Pattern* to learn how motifs were used to decorate yurts. In our own work, we used the children's designs from nature to make the decorative border.

For the first yurt, we read the children *The Tree That Reached the Sky*. The story reflects the Central Asiatic world of ideas with archetypal pictures and cosmological beliefs. From this tale, the children got ideas for decorations to use on the tent. They wanted to be able to "read" the tale from the designs on the tent. As they worked, the children were taught to tell stories and sing. As we rolled the felt, we practiced our singing and the stories that would be told when the yurt was finished. We also took time to split willow branches to make the frame and roof ring.

When the yurt was finished, we spent a day telling tales and singing in the yurt.

The second yurt was made at a farm in the city and was decorated with farm animals.

Storytelling yurt, made by children in England under the direction of Stephanie Bunn.

The children lay out their motifs for the storytelling yurt.

• 144 •

"Hattivatti" Workshop

"Hattivatti" was the name of a workshop that Stephanie Bunn gave to adults at Pohjois-Karjalan, Opisto, Finland in which the participants made wearable art using the techniques for felting a hat.

Stephanie's whimsical ideas are illustrated in her drawings.

The course participants already knew how to felt balls, tufts, pouches, and long ropes.

Stephanie encourages participants to use natural materials such as flowers, grass, and feathers in their felt.

The participants made wearable forms such as a mask in the form of a pouch,

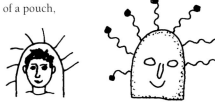

or a frontal mask.

Stephanie considers costumes to be skins that change. With the help of a mask, a head can appear to be *above* your head. For example, it can sit upon a rod high above your head!

The "head" need not be a head. It can also be a flower, a sun, a house, or whatever you want.

How to Create in a Group, or a Narrative on a Flower Felt

This project is appropriate for
- a school camp.
- an experienced class with the help of a teacher.
- a craft workshop.
- a preschool as a collaboration between parents and children.
- a course opener or finale.
- a family activity to create a felt or a carpet to use for a special occasion. For example, a birthday carpet, travel rug , car lap robe for Grandmother, or Grandfather's bedspread made by all the grandchildren.

All collective work should be a celebration, as demonstrated by the ancient Mongolians. But you can also work while you celebrate.

At the end of one-week courses in felting and painting at the Bäckedal Folk High School in Sveg, a celebration was held. Participants in the two workshops had been so busy that they had barely had time to speak with one another. On the last evening, a lamb roast was held down by the river on a pretty summer's evening.

As entertainment, we arranged the improvised felting of a picnic blanket. We took inspiration from the summer flowers around us. We cut open a striped duvet cover, dipped it in the river, and spread it out on top of a tarp. Then participants shaped dyed batts of fleece into their favorite flowers, dipped them into felting solution, and placed them face down on the cloth.

When the surface was filled with Här-jedalen's most beautiful flowers, the background was added. We used Swedish Fin and Rya wool left over from the course materials. First, we placed a thin layer of Swedish Fin wool on top of the flowers so that as many fibers as possible would attach to the background. Then came two layers of Rya wool, laid at right angles to each another, and the whole

Summer flowers of wet carded fleece assembled by both adults and children.

surface was sprinkled with fine drops of felting solution.

The other half of the duvet cover was folded over the wool, the tarp laid on top of it, and the whole packet was pressed down as we walked on it. To the magic sound of a mouth harp, we continued to press the wool as we danced a Finnish dance called the *jenka,* jumping a measured two steps forward and one step backward. When the crazy dance ended, we held onto each other and all stepped off the blanket. A chant consisting of the word "felt" in ten languages was read ceremoniously, and then, with silence and great excitement, the tarp was opened.

And there it was. Before our feet lay a gay white blanket, with all of the flowers looking up at us—wild pansies, bluebells. . . .

Of course, it wasn't complete after just a half hour of dancing and reciting a magical chant. We still had to roll it up in the tarp and secure it with rope, and then roll it back and forth with our feet. Pure Rya wool with just a few layers of Swedish Fin does not always felt imme-

diately, especially when the Rya wool is laid out in large carded batts with the fibers in parallel alignment. If we had started with carded batts of a blend of Rya and Swedish Fin, it would have taken half the time.

Jonny plays the mouth harp and everyone dances on the wool and tarp!

A few tips

If you want to make a carpet from a composition created on the spot by a diverse group of people, most of whom are beginners, consider the following tips:

- Choose a theme for the motif that is familiar to everyone and has a simple shape.

- Do not selectively alter any of the motifs that you believe to be inferior. In this type of group project, everyone must design as they wish. Or make it clear from the beginning that one person is chief designer. If that is the case, a design should be prepared ahead of time for the group.

- Ensure color harmony by supplying predyed wool. Otherwise, allow the participants to be free to create and compose as they see fit.

- If you fill the surface with designs, less successful designs will be less noticeable. Compositions that require design accuracy will take more time.

- Choose a wool that is easy to felt, for example a Swedish Fin/Rya blend, or Gute or Gotland wool, especially if you suspect that the participants may have low stamina.

The tarp is folded back . . . it is felt!

Glossary

The word *tova* is an antique Nordic word for the process of working warm soapy water into carded wool until the wool forms a cohesive fabric or garment. The word still exists in northern Sweden. The word tova also exists in Norway, Iceland, and the Faeroe Islands. The Finnish word, *houpa*, is also derived from the word tova. English synonyms are felting, fulling and milling.

When we say that we are going to felt, we refer to the entire process from carding the fleece to finishing the felt fabric. The felting process however, is made up of two steps: felting and fulling.

The original Swedish title of this book is *Tova*. Tovning is the term which was adopted as a name for the technique of felting wool fleece into cloth by Katarina Ågren.

Felt is the name for the end product. Felt is also in all of the Germanic languages and appears in the newer versions of ancient Swedish.

Felting is a synonym for tova; it means the whole process, from fleece to fabric. But it can also refer to the first part of the felting process, when soapy water is poured onto fleece and the wool is carefully molded into a loose cloth. "Well felted is half of the fulling" is an old saying that refers to this step of the felting process.

Fulling is synonymous with tovning, the term for the second step of the felting process. During fulling, the softly felted wool is rubbed vigorously to make it into a durable fabric. A grooved wooden washboard called a fulling board or *tovboard* is most commonly used for this process. Fulling is the same as milling—when woven wool fabric is beaten into vadmal. Both words are Germanic and their use in Sweden is a result of the German craftworkers who migrated to Sweden during the middle ages and Swedish journeymen who apprenticed in Germany at that time.

In this book, **tovning** has been translated as felting and used as a catch-all for the various methods which are associated with feltmaking.

Rubbing Technique is my term for the traditional Nordic method of fulling, where you rub the wool by hand until it becomes felt. I gave this technique a name to differentiate it from the Asiatic technique of rolling felt.

Rolling Technique is what I call the Asiatic method of fulling—the wool is not worked with the hands but is rolled in a supportive material until it becomes felt.

Resources

Books

Ågren, Katarina. *Tovning*. ICA bokförlag, 1976.

Andersson A. and A. Sandvall, eds. *Guldet från stäppen*. Lts förlag, Statens historiska museum/Medelhavsmuseet, 1979.

Andrews, Peter. *Nomad Tent Forms in the Middle East*. Vols 1 and 2, *Framed Tents*. Dr. Ludwig Reichert Verlag, 1994.

————. *The Felt Tent in Middle Asia: The Nomadic Tradition and its Interaction with Princely Tentage*. PhD thesis, University of London, Arts, School of Oriental and African Studies, Department of Art and Archaeology, 1980.

Artamonow, Michail I. *Treasures from Scythian Tombs in the Hermitage Museum*. Leningrad, London, 1969.

Burkett, Mary E. *The Art of the Felt Maker*. Abbot Hall Art Gallery, Kendal Cumbria, 1979.

Chabros, Krystyna. *Quilted Ornamentation on Mongol Felts*. Central Asiatic Journal 32, 1.

Damm, A., ed. *Langs silkevejen*. Moesgård Museum, Denmark, 1990.

Ekert, Marianne. *Lär dig tova*. ICA bokförlag, Västerås, 1985.

Engström, Ulla. *Arbeta med ull*. LTs förlag, Stockholm, 1978.

Evers, Inge. *Feltmaking, Techniques and Projects*. Lark Books, North Carolina, 1987.

Gordon, Beverly. *Feltmaking*. Watson-Guptill Publications, New York, 1980.

Gilberg, Rolf. *Shamaner og åndemanere*. Nationalmuseet, Köpenhamn, 1992.

Hellquist, Elof. *Svensk etymologisk ordbok*. Lund, 1966.

Herodotos. *Historia I–II*. Stockholm, 1968.

Hougen, Björn. *Snartemofunnene*. Oslo, 1935.

Hundt, H. J. *Gewebe und Filzfunde aus Haithabu*. Bericht 19, Neumünster, 1984.

Hägg, Inga. *Die Textilfunde aus dem Hafen von Haithabu*. Bericht 20, Neumünster, 1984.

Imperial Household Agency. *Treasures of Shōsō-in—North Section*. Asaki Shimbim Publishing, 5-3-2 Tusukiji, Chuoku, Tokyo 104-11, 1987.

Jettmar, Karl. *Art of the Steppes*. Crown Publishers, New York, 1967.

Keller, Richard. *Feutre*. D. Guéniot, 1990.

Kulturhistoriskt lexikon för nordisk medeltid del 4. Malmö, 1959.

Kulturhistoriskt lexikon för nordisk medeltid del 5. Malmö, 1960.

Larsson, Jr, Lennart. *Mattor från Kina, Siankiang och Tibet*. Interpublishing, Stockholm, 1985.

Mjeldheim, Liv. *Haus Selvhjelpskontor 1911–1961*. Vestlandske husflids- og husindustricentral.

Montell, Gösta. *Våra vänner på stäppen*. Lars Hökerbergs bokförlag, Stockholm, 1934.

Neilsen, Lene. *Mosekonens filtebog*. Skarvs husflidsboger, Holte, Denmark, 1986.

Olschki, Leonardo. *The Myth of Felt*. Berkely University of California Press, 1949.

Rudenko, Sergei I. *Frozen Tombs of Siberia: The Pazyryk Burials of Iron-Age Horsemen*. J M Dent & Sons, London, 1970.

Smådahl, Kirsten Julie. *Filting av ull*. Landbruksforlaget A/S, Norway, 1989.

Spark, Pat. *Fundamentals of Feltmaking*. Shuttle Craft Books, Washington, 1989.

Spark, Pat. *Scandinavian-Style Feltmaking. A Three-Dimensional Approach to Hats, Boots, Mittens and Other Useful Objects*. Shuttle Craft Books, Washington, 1992.

Svanbert, I. and E-C Ekström. *Mongolica Suecana, Bibliography of Swedish Books and Articles on Mongolia*. Centre for Multietnic Reserach, Uppsala University, 1988.

Trippett, Frank. *The First Horseman*. Time-Life Books, Virginia, 1974.

Magazines

CIBA Review. *Felt* vol. 11, no. 129 (Nov. 1958).

Echoes. International Feltmakers Association Journal. Mary Burkett, President, Isel Hall, Cockermouth, Cumbria, UK CA13 0QC.

Farkas, Ottó. *Der Syrmak aus Kasachstan*. Ornaments 1992/5.

Gervers, Veronica. *Methods of Treaditional Feltmaking in Anatolia and Iran*. Bulletin de Liason de Centre International D'Etude des Textiles Anciens, Lyon, 1974.

Grenander-Nyberg, G. *Filt I forntiden*. Folkets historia 1991/4.

Grima. The journal of the Danish felt association, Grims. Ulla Schubert, Den Gamle Skole, GL. Landevej 122 A, Marrebæk, Denmark.

Handwoven. Interweave Press, 201 East Fourth Street, Loveland, CO 80537.

Hemslöjden. Elisabeth Larsson, Kroka 7/9. 385 97 Söderåkra, Sweden.

Laufer, Berthold. *The Early History of Felt*. American Anthropologist, New Series 32, no. 1.

Meister, W. *Zur Geschichte des Filzteppichs im Jahrtausend n. Ohr. Ostasiatische Zeitschrift*, Neue Folge, Vols 10, 12, Berlin 1931–1936.

North American Felters' Network. Pat Spark, Ed., 1032 SW Washington Street, Albany, OR 97321.

Pakana 1/91. Pakanallissen Kirjallisuuden Edistämisseura, Finland.

Róna, -Tas A. *Feltmaking in Mongolia>* Acta Orientalia, Academiae Scientiarium hungaricae, Akademiai Kiadó, Budapest, 1963.

Shuttle, Spindle & Dyepot. The Handweavers Guild of America, 2402 University Avenue, Suite 702, St. Paul, MN 55114.

Spin·Off. Interweave Press, 201 East Fourth Street, Loveland, CO 80537.

Surface Design Journal. PO Box 20799, Oakland, CA 94620, vol. 18, no. 2.

Felt Organizations

International Feltmakers Association, Mary Burkett, President, Isel Hall, Cockermouth, Cumbria, UK CA13 0QC.

North American Felters' Network. Pat Spark, Ed., 1032 SW Washington Street, Albany, OR 97321.

Supplies

Carded batts and rovings

Ashford Handicraft, Ltd.
PO Box 474
Ashburton, New Zealand

Miriam Carter, Feltmaker
Charcoal Road
Dublin, NH 03444
Australian Merino. Sixteen fashion colors in carded batts. Send US $2.00 and SASE for sample and color card.

Fibrecrafts
Style Cottage, Lower Eashing
Godalming, Surrey GU7 2QD England
tel 01483 421853 fax 01483 419960

Louise Heite, Icelandic Wool
PO Box 53
Camden, DE 19934-0053
(800) 777-9665
Louise imports Icelandic wool in many forms, including roving.

R.H. Lindsay Co.
Wool Merchants
PO Box 218
Boston, MA 02124
(617) 288-1050
Dyed and carded romney fiber which is used by several felters I know. The fiber felts well, but not quickly.

Misty Mountain Farm
10266 Stillhouse Road
Delaplane, VA 22025
(800) 796-7746
Finn wool. Fast felting Finn wool from their own Finnsheep. White and natural colored. Dyed Finn fleece in six colorways. Felting batts in Finn, Finn-Angora and Finn-Mohair. Free Catalog.

Norsk Fjord Fiber
Noel A. Thurner
Rt. 2, Box 152
Lexington, GA 30648
(706) 743-5120
Noel imports Norwegian and Swedish wool. The Norwegian is Spelsau, the Swedish is Päls wool (Noel calls this Pälssau). Her carded batts are superb, and the fiber felts beautifully.

Quick Spin Wools
R.M.B. 1215, Shelford Road
Merideth 3333, Australia
tel 052 86-8334

Rovings
Box 192
Oakbank, MB, Canada R0E 1J0
(800) 266-5536
100% Australian Polwarth wool felting batts. Beautiful 20" × 72" felt batts, fine wool, natural and colored. Dyed and blends, rainbow batts available. Price list available.

Springwater Spinoffs
26045 S. Warnock Road
Estacada, OR 97023
(503) 630-4520
Merino and other fine fibers. In addition, will card your fleece.

Tynsell Handspinners
53 Cross Green Road
Dalton, Huddersfield
Yorkshire HD5 9XX, England

Wingham Wool Work
Freepost, 70 Main Street
Wentworth, Rotherham
SouthYorkshire S62 7BR, England
tel 0226 742926

Woodland Woolworks
262 S. Maple Street
PO Box 400
Yamhill, OR 97148-8420
(800) 547-3725
They carry many types of roving, batts, etc. including wonderful dyed silk bricks for making silk paper.

Drum Carders
Duncan Fiber Enterprises
21740 SE Edward Dr.
Clackamas, OR 97015
(503) 658-4066.
This carder can be ordered with both manual and electric control. It has medium fine teeth which work well for carding fine as well as other fleeces. It works especially nicely for color blending. The carder makes 16"-width batts.

Fricke Carders
8702 State Rd. 92
Granite Falls, WA 98252-9719
(360) 691-5779

Hedgehog Drum Carder
Meodene, Broadway Road
Mickleton, Glos., GL55 6PT, England
tel 01386 438349

Pat Green Carders
48793 Chilliwack Lake Rd.
Chilliwack, BC, Canada V4Z 1A6
(604) 858-6020

Dyes
Kemtex Craft Dyes
Tameside Business Park
Windmill Lane, Denton
Manchester M34 325 England
061 320 6505

Pro-Chem
Box 14
Somerset, MA 02726
(508) 676-3838
They carry many wool dyes and other products such as moth proofing chemicals.

Millinery Supplies
California Millinery Supply Co.
721 South Spring St.
Los Angeles, CA 90014
(213) 622-8746
Full range of millinery supplies, including stiffeners.

Paul Craig, Ltd.
Unit 3, Wealden Business Park
Farmingham Road, Crowborough
East Sussex TN6 2JR, England

The London Hat House
7 Kensington Mall
London W8 4EB, England

Frank's Cane & Rush Supply
7252 Heil Avenue
Huntington Beach, CA 92647
(714) 847-0707
Hat blocks.

Manny's Millinery Supply Co.
63 West 39th St.
New York, NY 10018
(212) 840-2235 or 2236
One of the largest suppliers in the US.

Felt Goods
Windsor Hollow Farm
205 Chase Pond Road
York, ME 03909
(207) 363-8163
Handcrafted hat blocks. Made from Maine Pine, many varieties of crowns and brims, all sizes. Custom orders welcome. For free brochure contact Jim and Kari Prichard.

Felting Supplies
Columbus Washboard Co., Inc.
1372 Qxley Rd.
Columbus, OH 43212
(800) 343-7967
This is the only washboard company in the US. Minimum order 6 washboards. Contact them for a dealer in your area.

Jean Lampe
1293 NW Wall #1501
Bend, OR 97701
(503) 389-3159
Wooden fulling boards and hand-held felting tools.

Index